Setting up a Strategic Communication Plan

# Setting up a Strategic Communication Plan

Marita Vos
José Otte
Paul Linders

Lemma Publishers – Utrecht – 2003

ISBN 90 5931 233 3
NUR 810

http://www.lemma.nl
infodesk@lemma.nl

Original title: *Communicatie & planning; het maken van een strategisch communicatieplan* (2002), ThiemeMeulenhoff, Utrecht/Zutphen.
Translated by Kathy den Boestert, 2003


Cover design and typography: Twin Design BV, Culemborg, the Netherlands

# Preface

This book is about strategic planning within communication. It is intended for students who are in the principal phase of higher education but additionally people already working within communication can consult this book whenever they need to devise a plan.

In order to align with actual practice, the book is made up of a six-stage communication plan. Special attention has been paid to the planning methodology as well as to the co-operative working required to formulate a good plan.

It is assumed that the reader already possesses a good knowledge of communication. Accordingly, it is not our intention to delve deeper into the theory or the core concepts of the communication literature. We can certainly imagine that some readers will require more background information. For that purpose, we have inserted the most important core concepts at the end of a section as well as placing a list of recommended literature at the back of the book for those requiring more comprehensive reading.

The School of Communication Management (SCOM), Faculty of Communication and Journalism, Utrecht University of Professional Education, has developed the study material for this book. The subject matter has been used for a number of years within various modules where students have made communication plans for complex practical cases, so that it has been thoroughly tested in practice. We would like to thank the many colleagues and students who have cast a critical eye over the contents and who have helped us to clearly define the stages within the communication plan. We also thank initiator Dymph van der Laan. We hope that this book will give the reader a clear framework for analysing communication problems. We also hope that it will stimulate the reader to invent his/her own creative solutions because, after all, a communication plan continues to be custom-made.

Marita Vos
José Otte
Paul Linders

May 2003

# Contents

# Introduction

In this book you will learn how to make communication policies and communication plans for an organisation. This could be for a company, a government organisation or a non-profit organisation. The approach from which communication policies are made can vary. It could relate to communication within the organisation as a whole (which we call 'concern communication') or to the internal communication for a company or business unit. Furthermore, you could think of marketing communication for products and services. The method presented in this book can be utilised for all types of communication specialisation.
The emphasis of the book lies on ***creating strategic communication plans*** for an organisation. Naturally, the story does not end there for the communication expert. After forming the plan, operational plans, such as sponsorship, advertising, or publicity plans, need to be put in place. However, these phases do not form part of the book.



### What is a communication policy?

Companies create policies in order to decrease sick leave, or to guarantee continuity, to improve profit or to become market leader, etc. The government, for example, creates policies to stimulate employment or reduce traffic jams on the motorways or to discourage misuse of social services, whereas non-profit organisations may create policies to improve their profile or work in a more market orientated manner.
Policies are created when you want to solve or prevent a problem. It could also be that you want to promote a favourable situation. A policy is an action plan: you state your objectives and you choose the way, the means, and the time required to achieve those objectives.
Policies are not created for small, everyday problems. Policies are created when there is a structural problem or when a problem could have significant consequences for an organisation, such as financial or personal consequences.

Policies are created when it is not directly clear what the problem is and also when a choice needs to made from several problem solutions.
As a communication expert, you will create communication policies. If you want to be able to create these policies, then you need to be well aware of the connection between the organisational policy and the communication policy. The communication policy forms part of the total organisational policy. The guidelines for the communication policy are always the organisational policy in which the objectives of the organisation are recorded. This book presents a ***staged plan*** for creating a communication policy. When discussing the staged plan, we regularly dwell upon the connection between the two policies.
Another theme that regularly reappears throughout the book is the connection between communication and other means of problem-solving. As a communications expert, you will need to feel at home with this link because communication is not always the correct means of tackling a problem.

### Communication planning

If you want to effectively approach a problem and develop policies, then it is very important to work systematically. Communication planning is a means of achieving this. By logically following stages, you approach the problem in a planned manner. Such an approach is the best guarantee for well thought-out solutions.



### Staged plans

You will find various staged plans in communication planning manuals and when you compare these plans, you will notice many similarities. In all staged plans, firstly the problem is studied and then it is defined (or redefined). Subsequently, the target groups and objectives are formulated and thereafter the plan of approach.

However, you will also notice differences between these staged plans. The most important differences stem from the fact that the staged plans are created for divergent objectives. Some staged plans are more focussed on creating multiple-year ***policy plans***, whereas others are created for ***project plans*** or ***operational plans*** for a fixed period, such as an advertising plan or a sponsorship plan. As you will have noticed from the text above, this book is focused upon creating policy plans.
▷ Policy plans, project plans, operational plans

The various planning methods do not all use the same terminology. Don't let yourself be distracted by this. A specific staged plan is an ***aid*** for systematically approaching a problem. This is more about the logical approach to the problem.

The ***main theme*** of this book is the staged plan which follows after this introduction. Furthermore, the chapter layout follows the numbering of the staged plan.
The staged plan begins with the assignment being allotted to the communication expert. Following this is the research and analysis stage whereby you research the situation and the context of the problem. This phase ends with the (re)formulation of the problem and the policy objectives. Thereafter, you need to focus your attention on the communicative side of the problem and determine the role that communication can play

**An overview of the plan:**

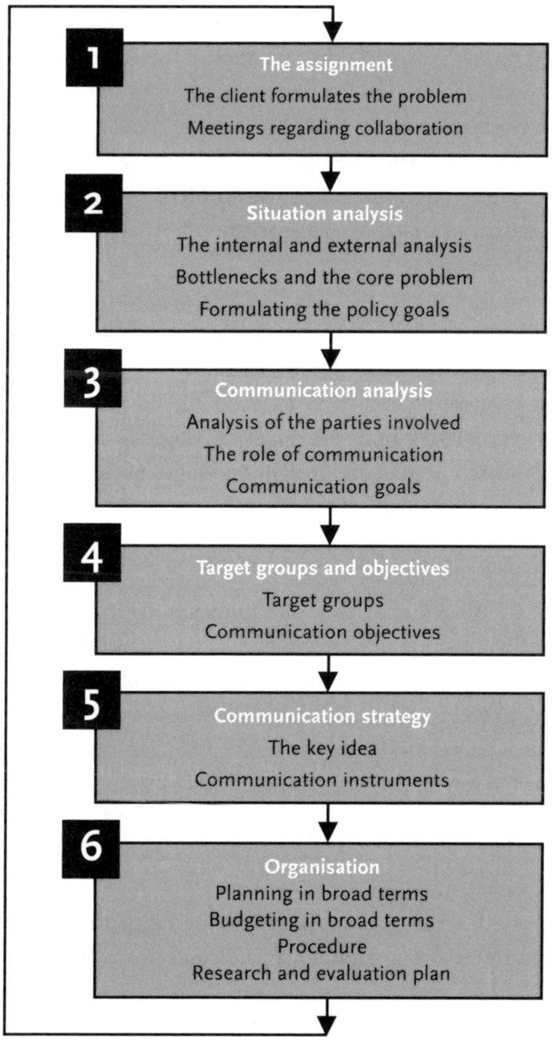

in solving the problem. If it plays an important role in the solution, then during the next stage, you need to determine the target groups and objectives and form the communication strategy. Once the client has approved your plan, you can then begin working out the operational aspects and only then can you start executing the plans.

## Cyclical process

Perhaps it now appears that you can find the solution yourself if you precisely work through the staged plan from beginning to end. However, it is not usually quite that simple. While developing the communication policy, for example during your research of the situation and the context of the problem, new facts may appear. In the meantime, the situation also can change and, just as important, your knowledge about the problem can increase at each subsequent stage. You are constantly obtaining a better insight into the situation and issues. Furthermore, you could discover that a decision in a later phase has consequences for a decision that you took during earlier stage. All this can result in you needing to change your approach to the problem. You literally need to take a step back and return to an earlier stage within the staged plan.



Developing a communication policy is not a simple, straightforward process where you begin at stage 1 and sail through to the final stage. Creating a communication policy is a ***cyclical process***. All the stages are connected to each other and each subsequent stage influences the outcome of the previous stage. This means that you need to keep a continuous eye on all the stages in the process when creating your plan. You will need to go through the stages of the plan several times.

### Practical cases

To help illustrate the staged plan, two case studies have been included. You will find the case study 'Waste policy' at the end of the book, whereas the 'Sugro' case study has been divided into sections. At the end of every chapter about a planning stage, you will find the associated section of this case.
The cases have not been worked out in detail. They are merely intended to be an illustration of the way of thinking in practical cases.

### Concepts

Creating a communication plan is the main theme of this book. With each stage you will come across a number of concepts from the communication

theory, such as identity, positioning strategy, and push/pull strategy. Accordingly, you will also need a supplementary theory about communication for each stage. You can well imagine that the quality of your communication plan is determined by the degree to which you succeed in bringing your other communication knowledge into the plan.
Providing this supplementary theory is not the objective of the book, but the theoretical concepts often mentioned at the end of a section can be your guide. The concepts come from the communication literature and are illustrated as follows:
▷ Concept

A list of recommended literature can be found at the back of the book, so that you can supplement your knowledge. Whilst working on the plan, you can ***look-up concepts*** (many books have an index at the back). Furthermore, you can use the theory to justify the choices made in your plan.

### Collaboration

A communication policy is never made alone, but always with other people within the organisation. It actually is very closely aligned with the organisation policy and the marketing policy. Accordingly, you will need to ***discuss your approach*** at regular intervals with the client, management, or parties concerned. With a systematic approach, you will build-in these discussion periods as discussions are necessary to ensure that you are on the right track and also to prevent your ideas and those of the client organisation from becoming too diverse from each other. Therefore, this book covers the collaboration between the client and the communication expert at every stage.



### Dare to deviate

The staged plan offers you a ***framework*** within which you can divide (the creation of) your communication plan into clear stages. However, you also need to be able to deviate from that framework if practice states otherwise. Furthermore, you do not need to cling rigidly to the staged titles (e.g. situation analysis and communication analysis). It is more important that the word usage in your plan corresponds to the language used by the organisation issuing the assignment.

### Tips

Within each chapter, you will also find a number of practical tips. These especially relate to the contact between the client and the communication expert. They can tell you how to obtain and keep the best possible collaboration.

# Stage 1 The Assignment

Creating a communication plan begins with a question, or rather with a problem whereby the expectation is that communication will play an important role in solving this. As a communication expert, you are generally presented with a problem although naturally it could also arise that you, as a communication specialist, take the initiative and bring a problem to the attention of the management of an organisation. The latter especially occurs when communication experts are employed within an organisation.

When creating a communication plan, it does not really matter who takes the initiative: a (potential) client or a communication expert. The stages that need to be gone through in order to obtain a communication plan are almost identical. However, there are certainly differences in the first stage, the assignment phase, where the assignment is given to the communication expert. It mainly concerns the differences in the preliminary assignment interview and the briefing. In this first chapter, we assume that you, as a communication expert, have been requested to provide your opinion of a client's problem.



In stage 1 when you, as the communication expert, receive the assignment, it is important to have empathy with your client. Place yourself in his or her perspective. Why does the client find it important to tackle the problem and why have you been approached rather than a specialist from another business area? In this stage, you need to understand the client's request as clearly as possible. Therefore you also need to understand what is the ***motive*** behind the request.

Before the communication expert and the client can agree upon the assignment and its execution, they need to have had meetings about the way they are going to collaborate. These meetings are planned at stage 1.

**Tip 1**
Take the time to brainstorm your project. What is the best procedure; what information do you need; in what direction should you be thinking? Use your connections and also consider aspects that probably do not have anything to do with the subject but did appear in the analysis. Note down your thoughts and do not restrict yourself. In any event, you can always adjust your notes and delete them.

For the procedure in stage 1, it doesn't matter whether you are an internal or external consultant. It is much more about the collaboration between the communication specialist and the client that is focussed upon the end result. The result has the form of a communication plan. An organisation can decide on ***outsourcing*** to a consultancy firm due to a shortage of manpower or because they don't have any in-house experts within that field. The construction of the communication plan won't be any different. However, an external firm will have more difficulty in relating to what is happening within the organisation than an in-house expert.

▷ Outsourcing



## 1.1 The client formulates the problem

At this stage you are presented with a problem, you are given the assignment, and you make an agreement about collaboration. It is quite possible that the client directly asks for a communication plan. It is also possible that you are asked for a recommendation or a proposal. Sometimes the client will ask you to execute a project or create communication aids. No matter what it is, it is always sensible to firstly ***draw up a plan***. The plan also ensures that you analyse the problem well, and above all that, you can easily discuss the different approaches. If the assignment does not yet call for 'the creation of a communication plan' but you think that it is really necessary, discuss this with the client. We assume that you and your client can agree on this point and that your assignment is now clear in this respect.

In order for stage 1 to progress well and to lay a good foundation for collaborating with the client, you need to build-in various 'discussion times'. The following scenario can act as a guideline for agreeing, continuing, and building-up client collaboration.

### The intake interview

The client has a problem and invites you to attend an initial discussion. Actually, he or she is not yet a client, but a potential client. The initiative for such a meeting can also come from you. In that event you approach the management on the basis of your own observations and advise that something should be done about a certain problem. If you are invited for an ***orientation interview***, ask what is the purpose of the meeting. Before the meeting it is advisable to gather information about the organisation, the product group, and the organisation's social circles.

If you are acting as an external communication expert, then you will generally need to exert more effort in preparing for this meeting than when you are internal. For example, consult the organisation's website, search for its annual report, and collect current information from the media.

### The briefing

The briefing is the meeting in which the (potential) client provides ***information about the problem*** so that you can judge whether you can help solve the problem. The briefing can also be partly given to you on paper. During the meeting, try to extract as much information as possible about the problem, the organisation, and the products. In order for you to judge whether you can help solve the problem, the briefing needs to be as comprehensive as possible. When concluding the meeting, what should be entirely clear is when the communication expert will deliver the debriefing, when the follow-up discussion is to take place, and what decisions will be taken then.

▷ Briefing



### The debriefing

Subsequently, you let the client know what you understand to be the problem. This is called the 'debriefing '. This is provided in writing in order to confirm the most important points and to prevent any misunderstanding about the assignment. The debriefing should state the reason and the core of the problem. In addition, the urgency should be mentioned in order to ascertain the timescales for making the communication plan available.

In this way the (still potential) client receives a ***report*** back and can see if you have understood the problem correctly and whether everything is clear. You can add a short list of questions concerning those aspects that you still have insufficient information about and which you really need to know in order to provide a good assessment of the nature and extent of the problem. For example, this could be the previous history of the project or precisely who was involved.

▷ Debriefing

### Discussing the debriefing

In the subsequent meeting, the debriefing is used as a guideline. As many as possible of ***those concerned*** with and involved in the project should attend this meeting. It is important that all those concerned in this meeting should agree about the nature and extent of the problem. It is then clear what point you are starting from and what the expectations are regarding the plan.

**Tip 2**

You can never be too customer-oriented. This means that you need to be totally adaptable, but have empathy with the client and their management vision. You do not only follow what your client does but you particularly try to understand why it is being done. Accordingly, your attitude during the discussions is extremely important. If you have three people sitting opposite you, look at each of them when you say something.



It is important in the early phase to determine whether it 'clicks' between the people concerned. When you work within an organisation, your client is usually a manager of the central organisation or a company subsidiary. When you are an external expert, it needs to click between you (or other team members if you work within a team) and the contact person who is acting on behalf of the organisation who allotted the assignment. The client's contact person is often a communication expert who works for the organisation. However, when an organisation does not have such an expert, it could be a line manager or someone with a central staff function. When there is a communication expert but he or she was not present at the first meeting, directly propose that the expert should be present at the debriefing.

If you feel that you cannot get on well with the contact person, take the appropriate steps as soon as possible. Perhaps one of your colleagues has less difficulty with the contact. In any event, you can discuss this problem but certainly not during the first meeting. Firstly, ensure that you analyse the situation well and discuss this with your team members.

During the debriefing, the approach to the problem will be discussed. At this point, it is not about the final solution to the problem but rather about ***the way in which*** you are planning to work towards it. As a communication expert, you present your initial considerations and staged plan for approaching the problem. Again, it is not about solutions to the problem but about the way in which you are going to work. For example, you may envisage a need to carry out extensive research or you may think you need a sounding-board group within the organisation to react upon elements within the plan. The client could then react and assess whether there is sufficient manpower and creativity within the team in order to operate successfully.

In addition, an alternative consideration is always recommended. This not only gets the discussion going, but it also gives the client and communication expert more possibilities when assessing which approach is most appropriate for the problem.

Furthermore, the ***budget*** needs to be discussed in detail. Firstly, the total amount should be ascertained. Creating a communication plan usually costs a lot of time together with research and travel costs. Discuss how you are to deal with any additional costs. These are all points that need to be made absolutely clear at an early stage. Finally, also ensure that there is clarity regarding the period within which the plan needs to be finalised.

▷ Budget

It is quite possible that all the issues cannot be discussed during one meeting or the client may perhaps first want to discuss things internally. In that event, arrange a subsequent meeting.

**Tip 3**

It is worthwhile giving prior consideration to the location where you will meet and to form an image of the people you will encounter. Always ensure that you have your business cards to hand. If someone else gives you their own card, do not put it away immediately but stop and look at it for a second or two.

### Granting the assignment

Following the debriefing, it will be clear how the client and yourself, as the communication expert, will co-operate. You should now define in writing, in broad terms, the project ***approach***. For each stage you need to signify within what timescales the stage needs to be realised, what people are involved, and the associated costs. When you anticipate that creating the communication plan is not too extensive a task, you can also mention a date when a subsequent stage of the communication plan will be ready for discussion. In any case, provide an estimate of the number of hours together with the total cost. Be very clear about additional costs such as VAT and travel and overnight costs.

The debriefing can take the form of an offer which the client signs for acceptance. The contract could also be one that needs signing by all concerned and should also define all the meetings. With a ***competitive bid***, various companies present their approach and tenders (for the assignment). The client subsequently makes a choice.

## 1.2 Collaboration meetings



Almost anything can happen during the collaborative process. Sometimes everything runs smoothly but it can also occur that people don't get along with each other and irritations arise. In order to ensure that collaboration goes as smoothly as possible, it is important to take stock of the situation in order to protect the intended result. That is why collaboration, in the aforementioned meetings, should be dealt with separately. During such meetings you could consider the following focal points.

### Contact persons

Within the communication department (if you are working for an organisation) or the company (if you are working externally), someone is appointed to be the primary contact person for the assignment. This is the ***account manager***. In this case, we assume this to be you. The client will also assign a contact person. Be sure to agree that this ***contact person*** has sufficient free time available to answer the communication expert's questions and can carry out discussions during the various stages of the communication plan. It is important for the contact persons to speak to each other within the short term. It should also be clear which people within the organisation could be

approached as ***informants***. For example, they could be senior colleagues who are familiar with the problem.
Sometimes a steering committee or sounding-board group is formed where progress can be discussed.

**Tip 4**
Be pro-active. Do not wait until the client gives you the information you require, but ask for it yourself. Remember that you are the expert and you know what information you need. Your client will appreciate it if you actively help him or her to think or sometimes even take the initiative. Try to assess just how far you can go with each situation.

### Forms of reporting

It should be known from the start who is to receive what information about the project and who is responsible for passing on this information. You should also be clear about the nature of the discussions and the reports that the client expects in the interim. Try to define these meetings as much as possible. It is also recommended that you produce a report or progress report following each contact with the client.



### Procedure and responsibilities

The collaboration between the parties should be written so that it is clear who is doing what at which time. Responsibilities should be made clear in advance in order to prevent any uncertainties (and with that irritations) during the course of the project. For example, when working with a sounding-board group, it should be clear, following the discussion, who owns the communication plan. If the comments from the sounding-board group are useful to you as a communication expert and it is your plan, then the group does not have to reach a consensus on each point.

### Consultancy role

In addition, it is advisable to agree about the ***expectation ideals*** that mutually exist. You need to obtain agreement with your client about the role you are going to play. When you create a consultancy based on your own professional insight, you won't automatically gain public support. When you work with a consensus and especially try to channel the internal discussions, these discussions do not usually follow your advice. When the client expects one thing from you and you do another, this leads to disappointment. We will explain this in more detail.

As a communication expert, you can take on various ***consultancy roles***. You can provide your expert opinion based upon information that has been collected, for example after having held interviews. With ***expert advice***, you recommend what is the best method for solving the problem. This role is referred to in the literature as the ***expert prescriber***.

▷ Consultancy roles, expert advice, expert prescriber

You can also act as a ***process facilitator***. In this role, you don't give advice to others but you help people within the organisation to think up the solutions for themselves. You assist with the process in order to reach a solution to the problem.

▷ Facilitator

A combination of both is also possible and often occurs in practice. You are then both consultant expert and process assistant. In this case, when creating a communication plan, you emphatically involve various people within the organisation at every step that needs to be taken in order to achieve the plan. These people are then closely involved in the choices that are made. This increases public support for the chosen solutions. Therefore, with a plan for internal communication, for example, you could set up a merger with a sounding-board group within the organisation.



**Tip 5**

At the start of the assignment, you need to extract as much information as quickly as possible. Therefore, ask for copies of all the information you are shown, e.g. overhead sheets, copies of reports, etc. Also check that the information is complete and who or what is the source. In this way you prevent the client from producing yet more new information at the debriefing and subsequently more after that. Try to ascertain whether the people and departments you can consult are the correct sources of information.

## Summary

At this first stage, the client's request has become clear. Following the briefing and debriefing, the communication expert has outlined a plan of approach which states what stages need to be gone through in order to find a solution to the problem. The approach has been confirmed in a contract. Furthermore, collaboration has also been discussed, including the contact persons, procedure and responsibilities, reporting, and discussion format. The expectations are clear to all. The real work can now begin.

## Stage 1 Sugro Group Case study

*The Assignment*

The sweet factory Holland Sweets (HS) is planning to merge with another company, Benem, who is also active in the confectionary market. The merged company wants to progress further with a more internationally sounding name: Sugro Group. New take-overs are not out of the question as a large number of smaller (family) companies operate in this market. According to expectations, there is only room for a limited number of large to very large businesses in the future.

Both companies are listed on the stock exchange. The share price is rising due to speculation about the forthcoming fusion and expectations are favourable. A firm of communication consultants is being sought because all these changes with respect to communicative consequences and chances, need to be seen.

Following the selection round, Communication Partners (CP) has been put forward. This firm is orienting itself for the assignment and has appointed an account manager who will explore the collaboration in discussions with the Sugro Group's contact person, the manager of the staff communication department. The firm is expected to provide expert advice in the form of a communication plan. The client and the consultancy firm have mutually agreed to have frequent contact. The firm has received a large file of documentation so that it can delve deeper into the client company and the market.

*To be continued ...*

# Stage 2 Situation Analysis

During the previous stage, the client presented you with a problem. Additionally you found out when discussions will take place between the client and the communication specialist.
Once the assignment is allocated, you can then proceed to the next stage – the situation analysis. During this stage you research, collect, and analyse information about the organisation and its environment. In this way you form as clear a picture as possible about the organisation and the situation in which it finds itself, by mapping out the context of the problem. You can't successfully solve problems if you don't understand the problems in the first place.

In this stage you search for answers to the following questions: What is the problem? What is the context of the problem? What is the cause of the problem? Does this problem have anything to do with other problems? This stage ends with (re)formulating both the problem and the policy objectives.



## Insight into the organisation and its environment

You need to have insight into an organisation and its environment in order to reach a good solution. This insight can be obtained through situation analysis which is important for the following reasons:

a You want to gain a good image of the problem. You need to know if the ***problem really*** is as the client has portrayed it; perhaps there are completely different underlying or associated problems.
▷ Situation analysis

Sometimes the client describes the problem as a clear communication problem. However, after more in-depth questioning, it actually appears that another problem needs to be solved first. For example, much more attention is needed on defining the market(s) because there is insufficient marketing information available on which to base a policy. Alternatively, the client has painted an image of good international collaboration between the organisations, while in reality it appears not to work so well.

**Tip 6**
In order to learn about the internal environment of a company, it is important to hold preferably the first, but in any event the second, meeting between the client and the account team at the client's location. You can then meet the people in their own work environment. Do the employees have their own offices? Is there a lot of noise from the restaurant? You can also gain much information by visiting the client at different times of the day. Do the people work late? Is the building virtually empty on Fridays?

b Only by having a good insight into the situation and a good diagnosis of the problem can you assess whether ***communication*** is the correct medium for solving the problem. It could appear from your research that the client does not actually have a communication problem but, for example, the quality of its products or services is unsatisfactory. In that case, the problem needs to be solved using other methods.

c An achievable communication plan should complement the situation and the organisation and should always contribute towards achieving the ***policy objectives*** of the organisation. Communication plans should align with the organisation's policy and take into consideration developments within the organisation's internal and external environment. If you don't take sufficient account of the context of the problem, there is a great chance that the client will not accept the communication plan. Examples are that it costs too much money or the solution does not fit within the organisation's culture, or the plan has little effect (it doesn't actually solve the problem) or it is counter-productive. Imagine having an internal communication programme that only increases the existing unrest and uncertainty. The cure is worse than the pain.



A communication plan is only effective and manageable if it fits within the organisation. Therefore, it is important to understand the organisation and its environment and you need to be seen to have a good impression of its ambience and culture. Furthermore, you need to pay attention to the management style as well as the environment and also the branch within which the client belongs. As an example, the health sector has a completely different ambience from that of the building trade.

### Situation analysis stages

A situation analysis consists of the following stages:
- An internal and external analysis.
- Co-ordinating the bottlenecks and formulating the core problem.
- Formulating the policy objectives.

Sometimes the client may provide all the information you need for the situation analysis in the briefing or upon allocating the assignment. You can then immediately focus your attention upon the next stage – the communication analysis. However, always ask yourself first how much of the information you need is already ***available***. Always be critical about this. Is the information offered objective enough? Is the information sufficiently complete and usable? Is the information still current?

## 2.1 Internal and external analysis

You describe the present position of the organisation in a situation analysis which always consists of an internal analysis of the organisation and an external analysis of the organisational environment. The issues that you focus your attention on depend upon the problem.
With a marketing communication problem, you need to research information and analyse, for example, market position, competitors, buying behaviour, and product image.
With an internal communication problem, your attention is focussed upon issues such as the organisational structure, culture, and management style.
With a concern communication problem, you need to be aware of the image of the organisation as a whole.

▷ Organisational structure, organisational culture, management style

### The internal analysis

You start with the internal analysis. Here you describe the most important ***objectives, standards*** and ***values*** of the organisation. What does the organisation want to achieve? What are the organisation's ambitions? What does the organisation consider to be important? How does the organisation deal with its colleagues, clients, shareholders, and society in general?

The most important objectives, standards, and values are often written in the organisation's ***mission statement***. In this document, the organisation describes in a nutshell how it sees itself, what it considers important, and what it wants to achieve in the future. The mission statement is a guideline for all managers and colleagues within the organisation.

▷ Mission statement, identity

A few examples of objectives and standards within a mission statement could be:

'We aim to be the best and most successful food supplier, not only with respect to the quality and innovation of our products, but also with the service provided to our customers.'

'We want to offer our shareholders a good return on their investment.'

'The customer is central in everything we do.'

'Our employees are honest in all their trading.'

During an internal analysis, you systematically research the functioning of an organisation. This leads to an overview of the strengths and weaknesses, especially with regard to things that the organisation can influence to a certain degree.



You can carry out an internal analysis at an organisational level as a whole (which we are discussing here) or, for example, at a business unit level.

You will find various summaries of organisational aspects in the literature that you can include in your analysis. Some summaries are very handy, but provide only a few aspects. Others are very detailed but are not very practical. An ideal summary doesn't really exist. You can add or omit aspects depending upon the situation and the problem. This also applies to the summary in Table 2.1.

Table 2.1 Aspects for internal analysis

| | |
|---|---|
| Product | quality, brand equity, assortment, production process |
| Logistics | information systems, quality and delivery of goods and services, supplier relationships, efficiency, stock control, distribution system |
| Technical | technical innovation, computerisation policy |
| Personnel | personnel policy; skills, quality and motivation of personnel, recruitment |
| Financial | financial policy, profit, turnover, productivity, capital ratios, load factor |
| Management | management control system, quality planning, capacity management |
| Organisation | organisational structure, organisational culture |
| Strategy | marketing policy, brand marketing, corporate image, product image, market share |

When creating the internal analysis, you need to be especially aware of the current ***developments*** within the organisation. You need to know which changes are important and play a role because it is often these changes that make it necessary to focus on communication.

The internal analysis provides you with insight into the functioning of the organisation. Furthermore, you need to form an image of the degree in which the organisation is similar to other organisations, or where it positively or negatively differentiates itself from other organisations, such as its competitors. You can then use this information again later, e.g., as a basis for creating a positioning strategy.



### Strengths and weaknesses

When do you consider an aspect of the situation to be a ***strength*** or a ***weakness***? That can be difficult. To start with, you should ask yourself whether the organisation is doing better or worse with a particular aspect than in the previous period. In addition, you should determine whether the organisation is stronger or weaker with respect to its competitors in that aspect. Finally, you need to ask yourself whether the business situation that you encounter positively or negatively contributes towards achieving the objectives of the organisation. An aspect is a ***strength*** when it positively contributes towards the objectives and it is a ***weakness*** when it detracts from achieving the objectives.

When assessing the strengths and weaknesses, you need to start from the assignment. For example, a strong culture could be an advantage (strength). All the employees are clear about how they should work and the way in which they should deal with agreements. However, a strong culture can also be a disadvantage (weakness). The company is so strictly organised that there is little or no room for new ideas.

### Information sources for the internal analysis

Where do you find the information you require for the internal analysis? You can gain knowledge and insight into the organisation by studying existing research (desk research), by consulting experts and sometimes also by carrying out additional research (field research).

For example, information sources for the internal analysis are policy plans, research reports (such as internal motivation research or image research) and a prior analysis of the organisation's strengths and weaknesses. Additionally, you can use annual reports and organisational charts. Furthermore, you can gain information from people in various managerial roles within the organisation. You can also retrace the history of the organisation or carry out research into the sector or branch, e.g. via branch and professional organisations. Sometimes it is not about the organisation as a whole but that more information on a company unit or product group is required.



### The external analysis

After having analysed the internal developments and the strengths and weaknesses, you then map out the external environment. Thereafter you research the developments within the environment that could have radical consequences for the organisation.

Firstly, it is to do with developments within the various public groups that directly relate to the organisation. This is the organisation's ***meso-environment***. It concerns important developments relating to consumers, competitors, suppliers, shareholders, capital investors, pressure groups, and the media.

The organisation cannot directly control the developments within these groups nor push them in the direction that it wants them to take. However, it can certainly try to influence the developments. Consider, for example, changes in the buying behaviour of the consumer or the confidence of the shareholder. Your attention is again focused upon the meso-environment in the communication analysis outlined in stage 3 (see Table 2.2).

▷ Meso-environment

Within the external analysis, in addition to the meso-environment, you will also research aspects of the ***macro-environment*** of an organisation. By doing this, you can consider the wider developments within society, such as those within the economy, demography, general environment, and culture. An individual organisation can't actually exercise any influence but it is certainly affected by these developments. For example, an organisation cannot exercise any influence on a recession, but a recession can certainly have a huge influence on the future of the organisation (see Table 2.3).

▷ Macro-environment

The same applies to the external analysis as for the internal analysis, i.e. there are very many developments that you could research. You will find various lists and checklists in the literature. Exactly which external developmental aspects you will research depends upon the situation and the problem. The reason being that you are carrying out an external analysis in order to gain a better insight into (the context of) the problem. If you anticipate that certain matters are not relevant to the problem, you do not need to research these. Furthermore, if additional information regarding technological changes doesn't provide you with a better insight into the problem and consumer behaviour does not have anything to do with it, then you need not include these aspects in your research.



**Tip 7**

Try and discover what trends are important. Build up contacts with independent research institutes and other organisations that can provide you with facts and figures about the sector. You can meet with people who specialise in trend watching and make enquiries at a society for communication experts or at an association of communication consultancy firms. You should also consult literature and publications in the media.

Table 2.2 Analysis meso-environment

The groups and developments within the external analysis of the meso-environment of the organisation that you can research are:

| | |
|---|---|
| Market | market share, market growth, market developments |
| Competition | activities, financial strategy, future competitors |
| Consumer | consumer behaviour, trends |
| Distribution | structure, power, service developments |
| Financiers | confidence, trends |
| Labour market | number of employees, professionalism of future personnel |
| Government | policy proposals, developing legislation |
| Media | changes in structure and financing |
| Pressure groups | influence, network |

It is important to establish what all the above-mentioned groups think about the organisation. We will delve deeper into this aspect in stage 3, which covers communication analysis. For example, it deals with name awareness, image, and social acceptance of the organisation.



Table 2.3 Analysis macro-environment

When analysing the macro-environment, the developments for research take place within the following areas:

| | |
|---|---|
| Demography | growth, extent, population composition, education level |
| Economy | buying power, inflation, international economical developments |
| Technology | information technology developments |
| Social/cultural factors | social relationships, controversial developments and emergence of new pressure groups |
| Judical/political factors | political climate, legislation, and international political developments |
| Infrastructure | transport, communication |
| Ecology | environment, climate |

It is important for you to realise that certain public groups can become more important for the organisation through developments within the meso and macro-environments. For example, the labour market can become scant due to demographic developments. The organisation then needs to exert more effort to find the correct employees.

### Opportunities and threats

When do you call a development within the organisational environment an opportunity and when is it a threat? The same development can have a different outcome for two organisations. For example, the government introduces stricter legislation regarding packaging materials. The company that foresaw these new developments has already adapted its production process to comply with these new requirements. It now has an advantage over its competitors who are still using the old packaging materials. The development is an opportunity for this company. The company that did not have its eye on these external developments must still adapt its production process. In addition to an in-depth revamping of its production process, this will cost the company a lot of time and money. Furthermore, an increasingly larger group of consumers will move away from this brand. The new legislation is a disadvantage for this company, so it is a threat.
In short, whether a development is an opportunity or a threat depends upon the influence it has on the functioning of the organisation.

▷ Opportunities, threats

### Information sources for the external analysis



Where do you find the information that you need for the external analysis? You can obtain knowledge and insight into the organisation's environment, particularly through desk research. For example, you can consult research that the client already has available, such as image and customer satisfaction investigations. In addition, trend reports and competitive analysis give an insight into changes within the market. Furthermore, you can consult trade literature and research that has been carried out by branch and professional organisations and independent bureaus for statistics, research institutes, and the government Ministry relating to Economic Affairs. The obtained material can be supplemented with field research by holding interviews, e.g., with specialists within the (branch) organisation.

▷ Preliminary investigation

### SWOT-matrix

The internal and external analysis can provide much information. The complete analysis is known as a ***SWOT analysis***. In order to bring structure to all your information, the results of the analysis are placed in a SWOT matrix which is a summary in the form of a table, divided into Strengths, Weaknesses, Opportunities, and Threats.

The SWOT matrix provides you with an insight into the strengths and weaknesses of the organisation as well as an image of the opportunities and threats within the environment (see Table 2.4).

▷ SWOT analysis

Table 2.4 Example SWOT matrix of a bedroom furniture supplier in which the largest consumer group is younger than 35.

| **Internal** | | **External** | |
|---|---|---|---|
| *Strengths* | *Weaknesses* | *Opportunities* | *Threats* |
| Product differentiation | Assortment not aligned to market trends | Growing market | New brands emerging |
| Quality image, value for money | | Rising demand<br>Increasing spending on interior<br>Consumer buying-power increasing | |
| Market leader | | | New 'me too' traders in the market<br>Aggressive market approach by competitors |
| Stock materials<br>Large/high costs | Long production time | | |
| Innovative production technology | | New plastics | |
| | Personnel shortage in production<br>Little relation to education | | Scant labour market<br>Reduced number of youngsters |
| Good position within bedding market | Distribution problem at warehouses | | |

The SWOT matrix is an aid to help you find your way within the stream of information you obtained via your research. It gives you an overview of the situation in which the organisation finds itself. You should realise that a SWOT analysis is not a goal. By carrying out the internal and external analysis, you are mapping out the context of the problem. Thus, the SWOT analysis is simply an aid to gaining insight into the situation in which the organisation finds itself.

You can find the organisation's problems within the weaknesses and threats. These need to be tackled, reduced, avoided, improved, or altered. The positive points can be found within the internal strengths and opportunities. The organisation can make use of these.

The internal strengths are laid alongside the external opportunities and threats. Thanks to the strengths, an organisation can perhaps avert a threat or put an opportunity to good use.
You do the same for the internal weaknesses – these are also laid alongside the external opportunities and threats. A weakness could lead to an organisation not being able to avert an external threat or make good use of a chance.

Accordingly, the internal and external factors are combined. This is achieved by assessing every strength individually and by ascertaining which opportunities and threats exist when these strengths are utilised. Undoubtedly, you will then come across interesting combinations.
Imagine that an organisation seems to have good growth possibilities abroad. It also appears that the employees are prepared to development themselves further through study and to live abroad (temporarily). The opportunities and internal strengths align well with each other.
An organisation's weaknesses usually relate to the financial situation. For example it appears that the market size will quickly decrease (threat). A weak financial situation combined with a reducing market possibly rules out any further development within that market.

**Tip 8**
It could happen that you discover that there is not really a communication problem but primarily an organisational problem. In this case, you should return the assignment. However, never do this without a good alternative and, where possible, provide names of relevant consultants.

You need to realise that a SWOT is a snapshot in time. With time, strengths can change into weaknesses and threats into opportunities. In addition, the SWOT matrix does not clarify which problems are the most important or which are the most urgent. Furthermore the co-relation between the various problems, their reasons, and consequences cannot directly be seen from the SWOT analysis. The matrix is an interim step that needs to be taken before you can begin further analysis.

The ***conclusions*** of the SWOT analysis, which are relevant for the communication plan, are included in your client report. That is the case when it appears from your research, for example, that certain public groups are going to play an important role for the organisation.

The complete findings of the SWOT analysis should not be included in your report. However, if you do want (partially) to include your findings, then put them as an attachment.

## 2.2 Bottlenecks and the core problem



Analysing the internal and external environment helps you to ascertain the organisation's core problem. You can achieve this by answering the following questions: Which problems are related to each other? Which bottlenecks have priority? What is the core problem? Who owns the problem? What are the reasons for the problem? Which factors influence the problem? What role does communication play in the core problem?

The first question: Which problems are related to each other?
The various bottlenecks (weaknesses and threats) and challenges (strengths and opportunities) which we came across in the SWOT analysis are not usually independent of each other. One problem usually relates to another. Therefore, you need to ask which problems specifically relate to each other and in what way. Are there perhaps questions from the SWOT analysis that combine to create bigger questions? Is a certain bottleneck the result of another bottleneck?

You can often cluster related bottlenecks together to make a larger whole. These are the so-called problem fields. In addition, you need to specify, as well as possible, if one problem is related to or is the result of or the cause of another problem. For example, one of the bottlenecks could be that the organisation is not very innovative although the market calls for faster innovation. Furthermore, its competitors are doing much better on this point. Due to this, the organisation threatens to acquire bigger problems. It also appears that the management style leaves little scope for the employees to come up with new ideas or plans and to participate.

The various bottlenecks can be clustered in different ways. For example, you can group them into short, medium, and long term or as internal or external. However, you always need to keep your eye on a number of key issues when doing this.

a Which bottlenecks have high ***priority***? What is the core problem? Urgent bottlenecks always have a higher priority than potential bottlenecks or those that only play a role in the long term. Bottlenecks that have significant effect upon the organisation have a higher priority than bottlenecks with relatively little effect.
Accordingly, it is essential to correctly define the main bottlenecks. If you actively tackle them, you will actually solve a large part of the problem.
As a communication expert, you will first discuss your formulated main problem or problem field with your client. An important condition for successfully solving the problem is that both the client and the communication expert need to have the same vision of the problem and the reason for it.



**Tip 9**
Various members of your account team are usually present at the discussions and presentations. Therefore, ensure that you have correctly divided the jobs among the right people when it comes to summarising, co-ordinating discussions, listening, posing questions, and reading body language. Then retrospectively evaluate what you have observed and experienced.

b Whose problem is it? Often there is more than one reason for a problem, so it is important to establish from what ***perspective*** you are looking at the problem. Top management, head of personnel, a production worker, and a communication adviser can all have different opinions as to why it is so difficult for the company to recruit personnel for the production department. That is why several different people can assess the extent, nature, cause and effects of a problem differently. Therefore, when you try to discover the cause of the problem, it is important to ask yourself; whose problem is it? To what part of the organisation does the problem belong and who is responsible for solving it? Top Management? A certain division?

c What ***causes*** can be attributed to the main problem? What factors influence the problem? What factors or developments worsen or lessen the problem? What is the interrelationship between the factors? Do they influence or cause each other?

An aid for obtaining a clearer view of the factors that influence the main problem (and each other) is to make a diagram of all the causes and effects. Firstly, you make a note of the problem and all the factors that relate to it. Subsequently, you indicate whether the factors are a cause or an effect of each other; whether they cause or influence the problem, or whether they result from the problem. Then, using arrows, you indicate the connection between the various factors and the problem (see Figure 2.1). Such a cause and effect diagram is also known as a causal (field) model.

▷ Causal analysis, causal model



Figure 2.1 Example of a causal model. The main problem in this diagram is noise pollution (also described in Section 3.1). In the figure the factors that influence the problem are shown.

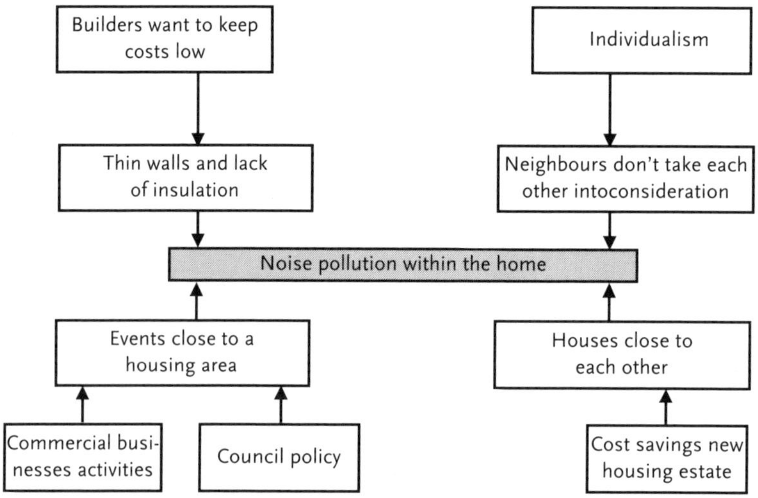

d What role does ***communication*** play in the main problem? What part has communication in the cause or consolidation of the problem? Do communication problems form part of the main problem? Is there, for example, a shortage of knowledge within an important group? Is it not possible to solve the problem because no effective discussions are taking place. Is there an ***image problem***? In short, what role does communication play in the process?
▷ Image

**Tip 10**

When you are working as a communication expert within a large organisation, it is worth realising that internal clients require just as much attention. Accordingly, you need to look at the departments and people who are involved in the project.

Such an analysis also provides you with an insight into what does and does not lie within the area of the communication expert. Some problems or developments can be influenced by communication, others cannot. If a service industry company wants its employees to provide more frequent after-care and service to its clients, it helps if the employees are motivated and trained in an internal campaign. However, another (non-communicative) factor can throw a spanner in the works. A heavy workload can prevent employees providing after-care and service as they already have their hands full with their normal work. In this case, when providing communication advice for an internal campaign, you also need to point out the necessity for tackling the workload.



Together with the client, you have now actually (re)formulated the problem. That resulted from

- the main problem that emerged following your analysis, and
- the inventory of factors that influenced this main problem.

## 2.3 Formulating the policy goal

The next task is to formulate the policy goal with the client. The policy goal is the organisation's answer to the problem. It states what the organisation wants to achieve in order to solve the problem and, accordingly, the policy goal formulates what the organisation wants to work on. Be aware that this is about a policy goal and not a communication goal.

Policy goals can vary from being broad to specific. It is important for a communication expert that the policy goals are as clear as possible. They need to be acceptable and achievable. A policy goal such as 'the market share must grow' or 'the living conditions in estate x must be improved' is too vague to work on. By how much must the market share grow? Within what timescales must the growth be realised? When have the living conditions actually improved?

By quantifying the policy goals, you know where you are as a communication expert. Examples of quantified policy goals are 'we will realise a market growth of 4% within 9 months', or 'within 2 years, 80% of the population will separate organic waste from the rest of the rubbish'.

It is not always easy to quantify policy goals. Sometimes the organisation needs to carry out an additional feasibility study of the plan. In other cases, the figures mentioned in the goal are based upon information gained from past experience.

Sometimes you may receive the formulation of the problem and the policy goal from the client's briefing, in which case you only need to cast a critical eye over it. In other cases, you must first carry out a thorough situation analysis in order to be able to formulate the central problem and the policy goal.



## Summary

In this stage you have seen that the approach to the problem begins with the situation analysis. This involves studying the organisation and the environment in order to gain insight into the organisation, the problem, and the environmental factors that influence this problem. You have also become familiar with the SWOT matrix and a cause and effect diagram. These are all aids that you use in order to bring some structure to the enormous amount of information that emerges from the internal and external analysis. The situation analysis ends with the extraction and description of the main problem and the formulation of the policy goal. In the next chapter you will study the role that communication can play when solving this problem.

Sometimes the client may provide you with all the information you need for the situation analysis during the briefing. In that case, you can directly move onto the next stage, the communication analysis. The situation analysis does not cover the contribution that communication can make towards solving the problem. That takes place in the following stage.

### Stage 2 Sugro Group case study (continued)

*Situation analysis*

The firm begins with an internal analysis of the Holland Sweets (HS) and Benem companies. Firstly, all the facts about the companies are listed.

- HS produces various sorts of sweets (with sugar, sugar-free, mint, and liquorice which are packaged individually, loose, and in tubes) and has international retail outlets. Its turnover is approximately 200 million Euros per year.
- Benem especially produces for the Dutch market and, in addition to the various popular liquorice sorts, it also has sugar-free liquorice, chewing gum, peppermint, and throat pastels. Its turnover is approximately 150 million Euros per year. Following the merger, a new company will exist with approximately 3000 employees.

From a SWOT-analysis of the companies, it appears that both companies will benefit from the merger. The SWOT-analysis is based upon an internal analysis and also an external analysis of developments within the confectionery market. This leads to the following conclusions.

- The merger is beneficial for Benem because it can profit from its future partner's (HS) good export channels, particularly for its wine gums and mints. hs is also strong in distribution within the grey market (automats, sport canteens, etc). Hardly any problems are expected with this expansion due to the large amount of expertise that is available.
- HS is interested in the merger because it can make use of the distribution channels that Benem has built up with chemists and pharmacies. HS wants to use these distribution channels for a new group of products – functional sweets. It has developed fruit toffees with extra vitamins, minerals, or calcium. Something similar has already been introduction within the Asian market, which takes account of dietary shortages there. Furthermore, HS also sees opportunities within the European market. Functional sweets can be seen as preventative aids against sickness and therefore are borderline with medicine. In addition, they are also considering producing a new chewing gum that is not only sugar-free but also neutralises acidity (which is necessary to prevent tooth decay through frequent use of cola or fruit juice).

In the short term, HS wants to build up their experience with this pH chewing gum by running a pilot project and the development of performance-enhancing 'smart sweets' has not been ruled out in the future.

The firm Communication Partners (CP) is now trying to clarify the bottlenecks, although people within the company prefer to talk about opportunities. What factors influence the situation?

- Within the capital market, the confidence that the two companies now have is very important; for the larger company, that is easier to maintain in the future. Favourable (financial) results are, of course, most important. Competitive developments need to be closely monitored.
- Internally, it is preferable that both companies find benefits from the merger. An efficiency boost is necessary but, due to the new activities (expanding exports and new products), this does not necessarily mean dismissals, although it will mean some relocation.
- When the confectionery market is expanded in the direction of preventative health aids, governmental legislation within this area certainly needs to be followed. 'Threats' could lie herein. Also, society's attitude with respect to food additives is influential as well as the attitude regarding health in general. The main problem therefore is realising the merger and utilising the resulting possibilities.



The policy goals now begin to stand out. Competition in the market is fierce. The Sugro Group wants to be a strong company that can play a leading role in future take-overs within the market. That is why achieving a good return is important. When restructuring the company (setting up new divisions following the merger) efficiency will also certainly need to be addressed. The company sees opportunities in market development (expanding exports with Benem products) and in product development (functional sweets). People want to maintain the already familiar brand names ('endorse identity' by naming the Sugro Group as the producer in small letters).

*To be continued ...*

# Stage 3 Communication Analysis

Within the communication analysis, you research the field of forces in which the organisation functions. With the aid of a role analysis, you make an inventory of the organisations and public groups involved with the problem and its solution. You research the information network and the information climate. The insight that you gain helps you to make choices in the subsequent stages: determining the target groups, objectives, and strategy. Furthermore, you investigate what role communication can play in solving the problem. Is communication the most important tool for solving the problem or can it be tackled better by using other policy instruments? You conclude this stage by formulating the general communication goals. Once completed, the communication expert's assignment is clear.



## 3.1 Analysis of the parties involved

In this stage, you gain clarity about the ***field of forces*** in which the client operates. You map out the ***involved parties***. Then you make an inventory of the public groups and organisations involved with the problem, which can relate to both internal and external parties. The result of your inventory forms a classified list (see Table 3.1). Within concern and internal communication, the involved parties are referred to as business relations. Within marketing communication, they are often known as 'stakeholders'.

▷ Field of forces, involved party analysis

**Tip 11**

A good consultant is constantly busy reflecting on and reconsidering what has happened. Follow up what has been said, evaluate the main points of the discussion, and assess your role therein. Deliberate over the questions that may be asked, then you will be well prepared for the discussion. Accordingly, be aware of the progress of the discussions at each phase.

What follows is an example of an 'interested parties list' with respect to communication regarding genetically modified food:

Table 3.1 Example of an 'interested parties' inventory

**The production column:**
- Seed suppliers
- Farmers
- Auctions
- World trade
- Process industry
- Intermediate trade and retail

**Governments and politics:**
- National governments and the European Union
- Politics of (inter)national organs
- Educational institutes such as universities

**Financiers:**
- Banks
- Shareholders

**Interest and Pressure Groups:**
- Pressure groups
- Consumer organisations
- Branch organisations

**General:**
- Consumers
- Schools
- Media



By creating this list, you illustrate the interested parties. You add an explanation of their realtion to the problem (are they very active and what is their message and approach). In the previous stage, the situation analysis, you analysed the problem and established what caused the problem (which factors). The key question within communication analysis is: which parties are concerned with the problem and who can play a role in solving it?

For example, if it concerns a socially related problem, then you need to know who to involve. You can often differentiate between the cause and the victim and point out which parties can contribute towards a solution.

Take 'alcohol and traffic' for example: the drunken drivers are the cause of the traffic accidents and the knocked-down cyclists, pedestrians, or other drivers are the victims. Catering businesses could contribute towards a solution by stimulating their customers to take a taxi.

With concern or internal communication, you will find supporters or helpers within your organisation but you will also identify opponents or objectors. Accordingly, you can then see who you should collaborate with in order to realise your plans.

Marketing communication would be more of a competitive analysis. Naturally, you would look at the competitors' communication approach, e.g. how related brands are being positioned. You can also assess who are the decision-makers and influencers within the companies (when the companies are the purchasers) or within families (when consumers are the purchasers). Who plays what role?

### Intermediaries

Supporters, opponents, and influencers are often intermediaries who inform or influence public groups. Accordingly, always look to see which ***intermediaries*** are involved with the problem. They form an intermediate link between the consumers and citizens.
They can be either individuals or organisations. Most people would probably consult their doctor about health issues or request information from the chemist on medication. Pupils can ask their dean about informative study material. Questions regarding technical equipment would be put to the retail businesses (shops and other distribution outlets). Companies can apply for information from their branch organisation.

You should also research how the intermediaries are set up. Are they active or passive and do they fill in the information themselves? What is their reputation with their 'supporters'? Some public groups are difficult to reach without utilising the intermediaries, e.g. this could apply to foreigners and old people. Sometimes public groups have more confidence in the intermediaries than in your client organisation. Furthermore, intermediaries can also have easier contact with the public group than the organisation. Accordingly, it is not always preferable to have direct communication from the organisation. Indirect communication via intermediaries can often be more effective. You could also consider a combination of both a direct and indirect approach. In marketing communication, you could try to reach the consumers directly but you could also have the retail businesses (shops) as a target group.



In this stage, you still do not make a definitive choice of the target groups but you do research who is involved in the problem and in what way, and who can play a role in solving it.

It is important to take the time to form an image of the (power) force surrounding the client. It is more about ***reflecting upon*** how your client stands within the environment. Try to take a fresh look at it. Ask yourself why other involved parties behave in this way. Try to look further as to what could be behind their behaviour. Possibly, other factors may play a role that you previously mentioned within the situation analysis in Chapter 2.

### The communication network

In order to gain more insight into the mutual relationships between the involved parties, you can define the ***communication network***. Furthermore, it encompasses who communicates with whom and what their objectives are. By thoroughly examining the communication network, it will become apparent that your client organisation does not have a monopoly on information, but that a majority of individuals and organisations are distributing information. All these individuals and organisations can exchange and distribute messages regarding 'the problem' and how to solve it. Some of them may think along the same lines as your client organisation but some will also oppose it. It is therefore extremely important to realise that you are not the only one communicating.

▷ Communication network



In order to clarify the communication network, you need to research which roles the various interested parties fulfil:

- the client;
- other (information) senders;
- intermediaries;
- receivers.

Accordingly, the ***client*** is not the only sender who is active in a certain subject. Imagine that the client is a factory situated within a town. In this case, ***other senders*** would include pressure and interest groups such as local environmental groups. They can weaken or strengthen the message that the client wants to publicise. ***Intermediaries*** are also actually senders. They form an intermediate link, but usually act independently. Journalists and the residents' committee are conceived to be intermediaries. Therefore, the client could decide to ensure that the intermediaries are well informed or to involve them when solving a problem. However, the way in which the intermediaries fulfil their role is dependent upon their own opinions and methods of working. The ***receivers*** of the message, e.g. residents, are not so passive as the word 'receiver' would have you believe. They are selective with such information and have their own interpretation of it. In another instance, receivers can also become senders, for example when they discuss the problem or the message with others. By investigating who communicates with whom, you can obtain a view of the communication network.

### The information climate

You also need to gain insight into the ***information climate***. The client's ***need to inform*** and also that of the other senders influences the information climate. The need to inform indicates how much they want to get a certain message over and what is their intention. Accordingly, the client needs to consider the other parties in the field.

What are also very important are the receivers' ***information requirements***. Is the subject relevant to the people who you want to reach? Are they interested in it or should you initially focus more attention on the subject? If it is a socially related problem, you should ask yourself if the people themselves see it as a problem. Perhaps they have a different opinion about the problem and its solution. If, for example, it concerns changes within an organisation or the introduction of a new product, then you need to investigate whether there are any obstacles. Sometimes resistance plays an impeding role and this initially needs to be mapped out. Finally, you need to ask yourself if the receivers in question are easily and seemingly accessible (consider language difficulties) and whether they are receptive to the information.

▷ Information climate



When information requirements are great, you can take advantage of people's ***search behaviour*** and, in particular, the freely accessible information such as the Internet (this is also called consultation). However, it could also be the case that information requirements are low. In that event, you need to ***actively offer*** information, e.g. via the mass media (we call this 'allocution'). Then you need to ask yourself if this actually is an fruitful business. Communication needs to be tailored as closely as possible to the information requirements of the receivers. It is they who determine the results of your effort. Sometimes it is better to choose an active approach via discussions (this is known as conversation). In this way, you could stimulate doctors to bring up the subject of abuse where necessary or you could ask ex-addicts to provide advice and guidance at schools.

▷ Consultation, allocution, conversation

**Tip 12**
It is advisable to produce a customer analysis, even when everything is progressing well. In this way, you try and gain as complete an image of the client as possible. What types of people appear as contact persons and how do they behave and react? What expectations are envisaged? The latter concerns the expectations that the client has regarding the project content, or the method and frequency of the progress report.

In stage 3, the communication analysis, an initial thorough investigation of the information climate is then appropriate because the information climate determines what you can further achieve using communication. You can subsequently make decisions in the following stages based upon the insight gained in Stage 3. When determining the target groups and objectives in Stage 4, you look in detail at the information requirements and the characteristics of the various target groups.

## 3.2 The role of communication



Communication is one of the instruments with which policies can be made. The policy objectives that you created in the situation analysis in Stage 2, do not yet state which instruments should be used for realising the policy. Sometimes the way in which you need to solve a problem and achieve your objectives are clearly defined. However, in most cases, you can achieve your goal in more ways than one and therefore you can utilise different instruments.
In general, the instruments used for creating policies are:

- enforcement (imposed, legal actions, regulations);
- engineering support (technical means, subsidies, facilities);
- education (communication);
- a combination of all of the above instruments.

These are also known as the three E's (Enforcement, Engineering, and Education).

For example, with a waste problem, the council can forbid people to dump rubbish in the woods; that is ***enforcement***. The council can also provide ***engineering support***, i.e. by placing glass bants. Furthermore, the council can deploy ***education*** by asking people, via an information campaign, to separate their rubbish into organic rubbish and other household rubbish.

A ***combination*** of instruments is often good to use in government communication when it concerns solving social problems. In addition, these instruments can also be used for internal communication. An employer can determine the rules for the workplace, such as everyone needs to be present at a certain time during workdays. However, an employer can also offer allowances, i.e. by introducing flexible working hours and opening the building earlier so that people can avoid traffic jams. Furthermore, the employer can deploy communication by asking managerial staff to discuss the departmental working times with the employees during work consultations.

You will also see a combination of policy instruments being used in marketing communication. You cannot really stimulate the sale of products and services sufficiently by using communication alone. An advertisement certainly advances the name recognition but to improve sales you also need to look at the product characteristics, the pricing, and the distribution (the other elements of the marketing mix).

**Tip 13**
Communication can bring parties together in order to gain a good organisational solution, or to communicate the discovered solution to the parties concerned. However, the supporting role that communication (or your team) has in this process, can be a different role from that which the client thought when he invited you in. Accordingly, clarify this with the client.



With concern communication you could consider 'joining' other people in the organisation's plans. Accordingly, working with communication alone is not enough because you need to co-operate with others. If a large stadium wants to organise more events in order to make the operation profitable, the government is more likely to grant permission for the events if they do not inconvenience the neighbours. The stadium is not able to impose measures on others, but it can certainly offer facilities and communicate. In order to minimise the traffic nuisance caused by visitors' cars, the stadium organised, in co-operation with public transport, combined tickets for travel and entrance to a football match. Furthermore, this was discussed with the residents. In this way, the stadium ensured that the residents received timely information about what they should expect.
Here, you can also see a combination of instruments being used, with one of them being communication.

Communication can also be used to influence knowledge, attitude, and behavioural patterns. You can also use it to initiate the communication process relating to solutions.
It is one of the policy instruments. Communication experts have the tendency to only focus upon communication for solving a problem while other instruments (facilities or measures) are sometimes more effective. Usually, a combination of instruments is necessary in order to achieve actual results.
You need to realise that the instruments for enforcement and engineering support are seldom deployed without being guided by communication (e.g. announcing a new policy).
▷ Communication as an instrument

The communication instrument can thus be deployed in two ways:
- communication as the main means and
- communication as a supportive means to other instruments.

Therefore, an important question is can you (partially) solve the problem with communication and, if you can, ***what contribution*** does communication make to the process. For example, if there is a lot of noise pollution in a neighbourhood, you can appeal to people through an information campaign to take to account the actions of the neighbours. An alternative that is possibly more effective is to increase the building standards. When walls are better insulated, less sound passes through them and that significantly decreases the noise pollution. Better insulation standards can be defined in stages. Perhaps communication then becomes necessary in order to lobby policy-makers to support stricter building standards. Communication can therefore contribute towards solving a problem in many ways.



### Interactive policy formation

Communication was previously deployed by governments particularly to inform people of the results after a policy was formulated. That still happens today, for example in the campaign regarding the introduction of the Euro. However nowadays communication is also deployed ***at an earlier stage*** of the policy process. Then the various parties involved in the problem get together to obtain an unambiguous problem definition and/or to reach a solution for the socially related problems. This timely involvement of the various parties in the policy process is known as ***interactive policy formation***.
The results of this process emerge from discussions or negotiations between

the parties concerned which can be useful in all phases of the policy process. This we call an interactive policy.

▷ Interactive policy formation

**Tip 14**

Sometimes it is sensible to deploy communication after an underlying problem (organisational, budgetary, or logistical) has been solved. Usually, you cannot do this yourself. Accordingly, you should immediately inform your client and ensure that your advice is well argued. If you have the name of an expert within this area who you can recommend, then you would be helping your client very much. Under no circumstances should you give advice or make suggestions outside your own professional area.

Communication consultants can further the quality of the interaction by thoroughly considering the information exchange, the phases of the process, and the preparations for the meeting. One result could be that companies from a certain sector mutually agree to voluntarily save energy. The government then does not need to (or to a lesser degree) embark upon a programme of regulation. Furthermore, the residents, companies, and schools of a particular district could jointly discuss the best way to tackle traffic safety in their area with the council. In this case, the communication expert is not concerned with bringing over a certain message but in furthering the quality of the ***process***. You are required to come up with a well thought-out subject for a communication project. For that purpose, it is necessary to have an insight into such communication processes.



Nowadays, government organisations more frequently apply interactive policy formation but ***other organisations can also*** utilise this method of working. For example, they could sit around the table in order to discuss internal problems with those concerned or with pressure groups. What is important is that the organisation has not proposed the solution already but is open to the views of others. Such forms of consultation are more likely if the involved parties realise that they are dependent upon each other for achieving a favourable outcome.

By now you should have a view of the role of communication in solving the problem within your plan. With that you can set down the definitive problem formulation and explicitly state the contribution of communication.

## 3.3 Communication goals

Now you need to generally formulate the communication goals. This is done in a few well-balanced sentences. These should include the ***actual assignment*** as given to the communication expert and what needs to be achieved with the deployment of communication.

A few examples of communication goals are:

- to ensure that people have an up-to-date image of the organisation and what the organisation stands for;
- to increase the feeling of belonging of the employees and those concerned within the whole of the organisation;
- to increase the category requirements or name recognition with the consumers.

When it is a complex or detailed assignment, you can split these communication goals into different areas: concern, internal, or marketing communication. For example, following a merger: to further the name recognition of the new organisation (concern communication), to guide the internal change project (internal communication), and to position the products of the new organisation as A-brands (marketing communication).



In fact, the communication goals illustrate how the communication expert views their assignment. Are they planning to distribute a certain message or create a subject for a communication project in order to get those involved around the table? What needs to be achieved by utilising communication?
By applying all the investigative forms, you now know that it is beneficial to utilise communication for this problem. The communication goals often appear to be different to your initial assignment. This is due to the insight you gained from the research done into the situation and communication analysis. In order to prevent any subsequent misunderstandings, it is very important to discuss the communication goals in detail with the client before you continue to complete the communication plan.

If you can summarise the communication goals in a few sentences, then you have what is known in the trade as 'a programme of requirements'. In this way upon completion there will be no more confusion.

In the following stages, you will create detailed objectives together with a draft for the target groups. After that you will put forward your communication strategy.

### Preconditions

In this stadium it may be necessary to propose a number of restrictions to begin with.
This specifically relates to:
- budgetary limitations;
- time restraints;
- juridical preconditions;
- ethical preconditions.

The ***budgetary limitations*** suppose that the communication proposal should not cost more than a given amount. The budget should fit within the total communication budget or within the budget of an organisational department. Within this, the priorities are set. The available budget for the communication activities in the plan must be realistic and the objectives must be achievable within it. If the objectives cannot be obtained within the available budget, then you need to discuss this with the client at this stage.



**Tip 15**
It is a waste of your time and effort to do research on issues that are already well known. Therefore, first look to see what knowledge, experience and expertise is already present within the organisation or branch. In this way you prevent employees from being presented with useless information or feeling that they have been bypassed.

The ***time restraints*** require that the communication plan should provide results within a certain period of time. They can come from the client who may want to introduce a new product for example, or other parties may cause them. It may also be due to a current information requirement from public groups for immediate information.

***Juridical preconditions*** relate to restrictions in the rules and regulations such as those concerning tobacco advertising, for example. Additionally, there is more frequently talk of self-regulating. In this case, a sector or branch makes mutual agreements whereby government regulations are deemed unnecessary.

Consider, for example, the Advertising Code Commission, which is the result of mutual agreement.
Accordingly, you need to ask yourself in advance whether you should consider juridical preconditions in the next stage in the plan.

***Ethical preconditions*** concern the standards and values of the receivers of the message; the standards proposed by the branch organisation and their acceptance by society. It is so that some multi-nationals looked critically upon the use of child labour in Third World countries. As a reaction to criticism, many companies have changed their policies and set up ethical codes.
The basic ethics of an organisation not only influence the behavioural choices of the organisation, but also the way in which communication takes form.
▷ Company ethics

Be sure to ask yourself which preconditions are important for your plan. If the client has not been clear about this, now is the time to clarify it. If necessary, you can propose having a 'preconditions discussion'. Later in the plan, this becomes more difficult as you are already well on your way towards completing the key elements of the plan.



## Summary

In Stage 2 (situation analysis) and Stage 3 (communication analysis) you carried out various forms of research. Firstly you analysed the organisation and the problem and then focussed upon communication. You looked for answers to a large number of questions. This will help you to make choices in the following stages.

In Stage 3, the communication analysis, you initially investigated the force within which the organisation functions. You stated which interested parties were important and outlined the information network and the information climate that you must work in. Subsequently, you investigated what contribution communication could make towards solving the problem. Then you translated this information into communication goals. Accordingly, the assignment for the communication expert has now become clear.

## Stage 3 Sugro Group case study (continued)

*Communication analysis*

The firm Communication Partners (CP) has managed to make the problems more concrete by splitting them up into three factors. Furthermore, the firm has also obtained knowledge of the specific aspects of this market. It is now time to do the communication analysis.

In order to obtain an analysis of the involved parties, the firm initially creates an overview of all the parties involved. Who are the competitors in the market and what public groups play a role? CP makes a list of the public groups such as the shareholders, the employees of both companies, trade unions, governments, and consumers. The forces are characterised by sharp competition; extra attention is required for the shareholders together with the intermediaries of the financial press. Furthermore, the communication network is mapped out. CP also analyses the information climate. There is a lot of interest in food and health. The company can take advantage of this by positioning its new functional sweets.

CP is now focusing upon the following question: What contribution can communication make towards solving the management problem regarding the merger? The deployment of communication as a policy instrument must specifically lead to an increase in name recognition and a better market position for the newly merged organisation.



CP proposes, in broad terms, the following general communication goals:
- Communication can confirm the confidence in the new organisation that the investors currently had in the two companies and possibly even increase it. The newly merged company must gain recognition.
- The change process must be guided with internal communication.
- The market for the new functional sweets must be opened up via a favourable product image.

CP is aware of the necessity to integrate communication with the preconditions and to ensure good mutual contact between the people within the Sugro Group responsible for concern, internal, and marketing communication.

*To be continued ...*

# Stage 4 Target Groups and Objectives

In stage 4, you establish your target groups and set your communication objectives. At this stage, many choices need to be made. Which target groups are the most important? Which target groups need to be approached first and which ones can be approached later? What exactly do you want to achieve with the target groups to help tackle the problem? In short, who needs to know what, when, and how?

The more you know about your target groups, the more you are able to determine achievable communication objectives. Therefore you also carry out a target group analysis in Stage 4 which outlines the most important characteristics and qualities of the target groups. By choosing the target groups and the communication objectives, you determine the problem approach. Stage 4 also provides the strategic policy guidelines for Stage 5.



## 4.1 Target groups

As a result of the involved party analysis, you now know which parties are involved with the problem and the role they will play. These were included in the overview you made in Stage 3. However, not all the parties involved in the problem are important target groups for communication when problem-solving. For example, competitors are certainly an important party to consider but they are not normally a target group for communication activities.

Using the information obtained from the interested party analysis, you firstly determine the ***primary communication target groups***. These groups are your main concern. By communicating with them, you expect to solve a large part of the problem. These are also the groups that need to be approached in the short term and that you expect to be successful. Primary target groups are the ultimate target groups, but they can also be intermediate target groups such as opinion leaders and the media.

In addition to primary target groups, you also need to define ***secondary communication target groups***. These are of secondary importance or are indirectly involved in solving the problem. For example, they are groups who are aware of the problem, feel closely involved, and would like to be informed about the (communication) approach to the problem. Secondary target groups can also include ultimate or intermediate target groups.

When determining the communication target groups, you need to be aware that a (marketing) communication target group is different to a (marketing) target group. The communication target group is frequently larger. For example, the majority of purchasing decisions involves more people who play various roles. The user of the product or service is not necessarily the same person as the purchaser. Those who took the initiative to buy are not necessarily the same people who made the final purchasing decision. The roles can be differentiated as follows: the initiator, the influencer, the decision-maker, the purchaser, and the user.

▷ Roles in decision making



Imagine that the marketing department of a computer games manufacturer wants to reach children aged between 10 and 12 years old (the marketing target group). From a communication viewpoint, the parents are also an important communication target group as they influence the child's playing behaviour and are often the ones who buy the computer games for their children. Another example can be found within business-to-business communication. When purchasing a heavy goods vehicle, different parties are involved: the driver, the financial director, the general director, and the maintenance manager. They all get together to make a joint decision regarding the purchase. This is known as a 'decision-making unit'. In this case, it is not sufficient to only inform the financial director.

**Tip 16**

It can occur that you have a fundamental difference of opinion with the client regarding the way in which you are approaching the communication problem. For example, the client does not have to agree with your solution. Accordingly, ensure that you put forward all your arguments for this solution and also mention why you do not see a way forward with the alternatives. Be as comprehensive as possible and try to consider all the alternatives. If the difference of opinion remains, then that is a shame but, in any case, you have done what had been expected of you.

The choice of communication objectives can also depend upon the marketing strategy employed. Are the commercial activities particularly focused upon the ***distribution channels***, such as the retail trade or the (end) user? These choices are consistent with the marketing preference for a push or pull strategy.

▷ Business partners, business chain, push ad pull strategy

The marketers of a Scottish whisky brand specifically employed a push strategy and aligned the communication strategy accordingly. Using shop displays, consumers were invited to participate in a competition with the main prize being an adventure in Scotland. Shopkeepers who actively brought this to the consumers' attention, received extra bonuses. Accordingly, this stimulated the distribution channels. By utilising a pull strategy, advertising would have formed the main part of the communication.

### Choice motivation

It is important to motivate your choice of target groups. Why did you choose a certain target group? Were there other possible alternatives, if so, why did you not choose them? When determining the target groups, the following considerations should be made:

- priority;
- urgency;
- feasibility;
- accessibility.

***Priority*** relates to the importance of the target group. A target group has priority when communicating with it can solve a large part of the problem. For example, if extensive road works need to be carried out on a busy motorway, you approach the large transport companies with a request to use an alternative route during a certain time.

***Urgency*** concerns the importance of communicating with a certain target group in the short term or whether it would be better to do this at a later stage. Some groups must be approached first, e.g. in a dangerous situation or because approaching this group first would make it easier to approach another target group at a later stage. Imagine that a city hospital cannot be reached via the normal route due to road works or other such obstacles. In this case, the ambulance crew would need to be the first group to be contacted.

***Feasibility*** relates to the chance of success. It is known that some target groups are interested in the subject, or are very positive about the organisation or product, or that they co-operatively want to work on solving the problem, whereas it is known that other groups don't want or are not able to support certain issues. Therefore, the results of your work will be most important to the first target group. For example, if you want to stimulate energy-savings by giving subsidies to people employing energy-saving measures, then you will achieve the most by firstly approaching the people who have an affinity with it. Possibly their behaviour will stimulate others later.

***Accessibility*** concerns the contact with the target group. Some groups can easily be reached with communication because you know where they live or which media they use, whereas others are very difficult to reach. Therefore, you would begin school fund-raising by contacting old students whose addresses you have, as they are the easiest to reach. There could also be reasons why some groups are more difficult to reach, e.g. because there may be a language barrier. Alternatively, the people who belong to the target group may have few common characteristics and may use very different types of media.



Take this as an example. Imagine that the approach to child abuse is to focus upon making the subject more discussible, quicker to spot, and to deal more quickly with notified cases. The final target groups, the children and the abusers, are difficult to identify. You do not know who they are beforehand. Above all, the group has few common characteristics because abuse appears in all levels of society ***(accessibility)***. However, you still want to reach these abusers. In this case, you can focus upon family doctors and teachers. Then you need to take the following into consideration: doctors and teachers have contact with both parents and children who are victims. Therefore, as an intermediary target group, they have a very important position in the social network. Many members of the ultimate target group (children and abusers) can be reached via these intermediaries ***(priority)***. The following considerations should also be noted: If doctors and teachers do not know how to deal with signs of child abuse, they can certainly hinder the abused children from expressing themselves (***urgency***). Finally, co-operation can be expected from doctors and teachers because notifying child abuse is closely related to their job responsibilities ***(feasibility)***.

**Tip 17**
When you work with different clients on the same project, you need to make clear agreements. Who is the primary client, in other words, who is the final assessor and decision-maker? Furthermore, how does the invoicing take place or, rather, to whom do you send the invoice with the specification?

### Target group analysis

The more you know about the target groups, the better you are at determining the communication objectives. Within the target group analysis, you research and describe the most important characteristics and attributes of the groups.
▷ Target groups, characteristics

Usually, there is already some information available about the target groups, based upon the client's knowledge and experience. However, do ask yourself if the client's information is current, sufficiently complete, and objective. Furthermore, you also collected relevant information yourself during the swot, interested party and communication analysis.



However, in most cases you will need to consult additional sources, such as third-party market research or statistical information from the Central Bureau of Statistics. Often you will come to the conclusion that additional field research is required because you have insufficient knowledge about the target groups to determine the objectives and strategy.
***Additional research*** could be necessary in order to be able to map out the knowledge and behavioural characteristics of the target groups. It is important to define well their specific characteristics and attributes with your client.

When determining the target groups and objectives, you should initially work generally and then later more specifically. Firstly, you globally ***describe*** the target groups. Using internal groups as an example, you would distinguish between the top management, middle management, and employees. It may be necessary to make further distinctions between these groups. Accordingly, you need to look at the target groups again in order to give each target group as exact a description as possible. Dependent upon the problem, it may be necessary to differentiate between age, department, or division, or whether they are production or officer workers.

Take this example. For internal communication regarding the re-organisation of an industrial company, it may be important to make distinctions between the various company divisions such as the metal division where many changes take place and the aluminium division with relatively fewer changes. Alternatively, it could be a division in England where many changes need to be made and a division in the Netherlands where fewer changes are foreseen.

You can often distinguish various sections within a target group, so you need to ask yourself whether you need to segment the target groups. They need to be segmented when the start situation, or the relevant characteristics, or the information search behaviour, or the media use within a target group is different. In other words, when the foreknowledge or attitude regarding the problem differs. Due to this, the communicative approach for the segments will also be different. Not only can the message be different for the various ***segments*** (or subgroups) but also the instruments and media used. You only know once you have analysed the target group whether segments within the group need to be differentiated.

▷ Target group segmentation



If the target groups consist of different segments, what do the segments look like?

What ***criteria*** are your sub-divisions based upon? By segmenting and focusing upon the characteristics of the target groups, you can answer the following questions:

- How big are the (sub) target groups? The size of the target group is important for the way in which it is going to be approached (personally, or via the mass media).
- How homogeneous is the target group? Can the target group be considered as a whole or does it consist of various target groups (segments) which differ from each other on relevant points? You need this knowledge in order to decide upon the message and means to be used for the segmentation.
- What characteristics do the target groups have? This concerns the characteristics that are important for achieving the communication objectives.

You can now work through the following key points:

- Does the target group need to be split into relevant demographic characteristics such as age and location?

- Are there important social-economical characteristics such as education, income, and family structure?
- Sometimes the demographical and social-economical characteristics are so diverse that you would do better to look at lifestyles or motives (also known as 'drives' in the literature).

Additionally, you need to look at knowledge, attitude, and behaviour.
- What are the important knowledge attributes? The following questions could be useful: What does the target group know about the subject? What does the target group know about the sender? What information requirements does the target group have?
- Other knowledge factors are also important, e.g.: To what degree is the target group able to spot, gather, retain, and reproduce information?
- What are the important attitude characteristics?
  In this case, relevant questions could be: What interests does the target group have? What is the attitude and involvement of the target group regarding the subject and the sector within which it appears? Does the target group consider the problem as its own (involvement)?
  ▷ (Low/high) involvement
  Does the (sub) target group have an expressed opinion about the subject? Is the target group interested in the problem? To what degree is the target group open to solutions to the problem? What does the target group have in terms of time, money, participation, etc., in order to solve the problem? What attitude does the target group have regarding the sender? How much confidence do they have in the sender?
- What are the important behavioural and activity characteristics? This relates to questions such as: What behavioural patterns are characteristic of the target group? How is the target group dealing with the problem? For example, how often does the (sub) target group make use of a product or service and in what way? Try to differentiate between the use that a consumer makes of a product category and a particular brand. For example, focus upon users of a product category who usually choose another brand.
- Other questions that could be of importance here are: What do the members of the target group do in their spare time? Do they have behavioural activities that could be relevant in reaching them? Could they be reached in their spare time at discos, sport associations, or religious gathering?

- Are there any other relevant characteristics such as ownership (e.g. a computer or a car) or distinguishing standards and values?

Additionally, the target group's media use, information search behaviour, and communication network is important information for determining the objectives and as a basis for the communication strategy. It can also be important for segmenting the target group.

- Media use: What media does the (sub) target group use? In other words, what do the members of the target group read, look at, and listen to? When do they do this and how often do they do it?
- Communication network: In which communication network is the (sub) target group active? Who do the members of the group have contact with and who do they consider to be opinion leaders?
- Information search behaviour: Where do the (sub) target group look for information about the subject? Do the members of the target group search for the information themselves? Do they put a lot of effort into obtaining the information or does the information need to be handed to them on a plate?



However, be aware that all of the above-mentioned personal characteristics are not important for each and every communication questionnaire. Accordingly, before proceeding with further research, determine which characteristics are relevant and keep to those. Before deciding to do further research, always use information from existing research.

Subsequently, provide an overview of the entire (sub) target groups with their most relevant qualities and characteristics. The specified target groups should be:

- ***large enough***. Working with too small a group costs a lot of time and effort.
- ***sufficiently homogeneous*** on the critical points. In any event, the target group needs to have several relevant common characteristics.
- ***sufficiently accessible***. Communication instruments and methods can only be employed once you know if and how you can reach the target group.

It is important to discuss the (sub) target groups and their relevant characteristics with your client. The client organisation and yourself as the communication specialist, must be in agreement in order to avoid any misunderstandings with additional research and in determining the objectives.

**Tip 18**

By communicating well with your client, you develop a shared knowledge. Plenty of discussion creates a foundation for your plan with the client. In this way, the quality of your communication advice increases.

## 4.2 Communication objectives

In the 'Analysis of the Parties involved' in Stage 3, you determined general communication objectives in order to indicate what contribution communication made towards solving the problem. An example of a communication objective in general is 'preparing the personnel for a merger'. After determining the target groups, you then set the (more detailed) communication objectives. The objectives for the personnel could be 'that they know why the merger is necessary, that they understand what steps are going to be taken and become interested in the company to be merged.

Communication objectives provide as accurately as possible what you want to achieve with a certain target group in the future. Communication is utilised when you want to change something in people or to retain something. That 'something' can be very different. It could be to retain or change the level of knowledge, attitude, and behaviour. An objective relates to the final situation. It is the situation that you want to achieve using communication.



In order to create a realistic objective, you need to know what the current (or start) situation is, as you want to turn this into the final situation using communication. Communication objectives are formulated in terms of what the target group needs to know, want, feel, find, be able to or do within a certain period. Accordingly, objectives can be very different.

▷ Communication objectives

***Knowledge-based objectives*** mainly concern:

- public awareness of an organisation or brand;
- knowledge about an organisation or brand (positioning);
- knowledge of a certain subject or problem.

***Attitude objectives*** mainly concern:

- attitude with respect to an organisation or brand, e.g. involvement;
- interest shown in a certain subject or the awareness of a problem;

- being aware of a need in a product category;
- satisfaction, e.g. after a sale.

***Behavioural objectives*** mainly concern:
- behavioural intentions regarding an organisation, brand, or particular problem;
- information request concerning an organisation, brand, or particular problem;
- possessing skills, e.g. communicative skills.

If the objective relates to attitude, then normally an educational / knowledge-based objective is also formulated. If the objective relates to behaviour (this is not always the case), then both educational and attitude objectives are formulated. An individual set with communication objectives is usually created for each target group.
Behavioural objectives for concern communication can quickly sound rather manipulative so then perhaps educational and attitude objectives would suffice. With internal communication, behavioural objectives could be communicative skills that increase the employees customer focus. Within marketing communication, you could strive to maintain the customer's preference for a certain brand. Whether their buying behaviour would change as a result is dependent upon other elements of the marketing mix, such as the product characteristics, distribution (availability), and price.



Once you have reached agreement with the client regarding the objectives, the choice of strategy and discussion often becomes easier. After devising the strategy in Stage 5, you then check to see whether all the objectives from Stage 4 can actually be achieved. It often appears that some of the objectives still need to be covered by an adequate strategy.
Again you will see that creating a communication plan is not a linear but a circular process. All the stages interrelate with each other. Subsequent stages influence the results of earlier stages. Accordingly, you will need to go through the various stages many times and then you will gain more clarity.

Objectives are the ***criteria*** used for determining the success of the communication effort. When can you confirm that the communication effort has been rewarding and successful? What effect then needs to be achieved by communication with the target group?
If you do not determine in advance what you want the communication effort to achieve, then you are also unable to confirm retrospectively whether the desired effect was actually achieved using communication.

## Criteria for communication objectives

Communication objectives must conform to the following requirements. They must be concrete, quantified, timed, and measurable.
***Concrete*** means that the objective must describe what effect, with respect to knowledge, attitude, and behaviour, needs to be obtained from the target group.
***Quantified*** means that the objective must state the percentage of people within the target group who must be effected.
***Timed*** means that the objective must state when the effect needs to be achieved or not.
***Measurable*** means that the objective must be formulated in such a way that it can be assessed retrospectively whether the effect on the target group was achieved or not.

An example of a badly formulated communication objective is as follows:
'Many people will shortly know a lot more about energy-saving'. This objective is neither concrete nor qualified and it is clearly not timed. You do not know when and by whom this needs to be achieved. There is no way you could determine the strategy and communication instruments with such a vague objective. Furthermore, you are unable to determine retrospectively whether the objective has been achieved or not. This objective is also not measurable.
The following communication objectives do conform to the required criteria:
- '60% of employees will endorse the need for reorganisation by May 1, next year' and
- '70% of library users aged 50 years and over will know within two months of the start of the communication campaign how they can independently log loaned items into the electronic lending system'.

It is important to pay sufficient attention to objectives as they provide you with guidelines for a further ***approach*** to the problem, wherein you can confirm what you want to achieve with which target group. Only when you know what you want to achieve and are familiar with the target groups, can you determine how you are going to achieve it and which strategy you are going to employ. Therefore, the choice of target groups and objectives in stage 4 determines the communicative approach in Stage 5.
The communication strategy is the answer to the pursued objectives for the target groups. Therefore, make sure that you do not propose strategy choices in Stage 4. You first need to have your objectives in order to substantiate a good choice of strategy.

A good objective also needs to be ***realistic***. The ambition level of the objective must not be higher (or lower) than what you actually expect to be able to achieve within the target group. In addition, you need to realise that communication costs money. Communication implementation must be done as efficiently and effectively as possible and the ambition level of the communication objective must also fit within the available budget. A small budget often means that one cannot be too ambitious.

Another reason why objectives need to be as precise as possible is that they are measurements for ***retrospectively*** determining the success of the communication effort. Accordingly, objectives must be precise and measurable. If they are not, then you will be unable to ascertain what you have achieved with communication. This is also known as 'accountability', which is justifying the effects you have achieved with the effort made.

When a communication project continues for a longer period, you also need to make interim measurements to ascertain the extent to which the objectives are being achieved. For this purpose, you can establish interim stages. For example, you differentiate between objectives that need to be achieved within two years, but you also provide ***interim objectives*** that must be achieved within a year. The results of these interim measurements can lead to amendments in the communication plan, such as in the strategy.



**Tip 19**
Regularly place 'collaboration' on the agenda during your contact with the client. It offers both parties the opportunity to delve further into the attitude, expectations, and details of the collaboration. Furthermore, other seemingly indirect subjects can also come up for discussion, such as planning, invoicing, team players, accessibility, and availability of (confidential) information.

Communication is often employed with other instruments, such as facilities, subsidies, or fines, or in marketing with price and distribution. If you envisage that the effects of communication are going to be difficult to isolate retrospectively from the influence of the other instruments, then pay extra attention to formulating the communication objectives. In particular, behavioural objectives, such as buying behaviour, can often pose difficulties.
In this connection, be aware that a marketing objective is not a communication

objective. An example marketing objective is: 'within six months, sales of the Lifeloft product will increase by 10% within the 15-25 years age group'. A marketing objective is much broader than a communication objective and is obtained by using more instruments than communication alone. An example communication objective would be: 'within six months, Lifelot's brand awareness will increase by 45% within the 15-25 years age group'.

During this stage, you state what objectives you want to achieve within the target groups. These are ***effect objectives***. At a later stage, once the strategy is determined, you can develop them as operational plans into process and medium objectives. Process objectives relate to the processing of the expressed communication by the receivers. For example, you want to know whether the target group understands the folder and remembers the advert. Medium objectives relate to the receiver's contact with the expressed communication. How often have the target group seen a particular advert? These objectives are narrower than the communication objectives. You can also formulate these at a later stage once you have determined the strategy, instruments, specific methods, and media to be employed.

Therefore the communication objectives you formulated in stage 4 are objectives that describe a particular ***effect*** upon the target groups with respect to knowledge, attitude, and behaviour.



**Tip 20**

When making an inventory of the bottlenecks, you need to prioritise them. Firstly, draw up a list and subsequently go through them with the client. In this way, it becomes clear what needs to be emphasised. You contribute new ideas and, at the same time, you utilise the knowledge and experience of your client.

### From general to specific

When determining ***objectives***, you work in the same way as when determining target groups. You work from general to specific. First you determine what you want to achieve with the (primary) target groups. This is made as definite as possible, but you do not yet need to adhere to all the demands required for a good objective. Only later do you need to determine precisely what you want to achieve with the different segments.

Here is an example limited to objectives at a knowledge-based level. Consider that a new medicine is shortly to be introduced into the market for heart patients. The medicine can have side-effects for patients with liver abnormalities. The primary target groups are the medical staff and the dispensing chemists. Firstly, you need to formulate the general communication objectives.

- Medical staff treating heart patients and issuing prescriptions are aware of the new medicine before its introduction and know that it can have side-effects for patients with liver abnormalities.
- All dispensing chemists are aware of the new medicine one month before its introduction and know that it can have side-effects for patients with liver abnormalities.

Subsequently, you develop the objectives further into measurable objectives for the various segments. For example:

- One month before its introduction, 80% of the family doctors in the Netherlands without their own pharmacy are aware of the side-effects of the medicine for heart patients.

Sometimes a policy plan can run for several years and, for its development, relies upon the ***project plans*** that are formulated. In this case, the main focus of the plan needs to be clear although the objectives do not need to be so detailed as all the details are included in the project plans.



### Substantiate the objectives

Communication objectives are always determined together with your client. Whose acceptance is extremely important, as discussing the objectives can lead to further discussions. For example, you may find that the client's ambition level is not realistic or that it is disproportionate to the available budget.

Clients have the tendency to attribute too much influencing value to communication. The client wants a behavioural change while you, as the communication specialist, estimate that in the forthcoming period, the most feasible is to conserve behaviour or gain a conscious change within a limited section of the target group. Therefore, justify and discuss the choices made. Otherwise the expectations regarding the results of the communication effort will be out of line.

The same applies when substantiating the objectives as for substantiating the target groups. Explain explicitly why you chose certain objectives, what the alternatives were, and why you decided not to choose those alternatives.

## Overview of target groups and objectives

Now you need to display the target groups and objectives in a clear ***diagram*** (see Table 4.1). If further communication problems play a role, then provide an overview of the target groups and objectives for each problem. Try to find logical divisions within the target groups, such as concern, internal, and marketing communication target groups.

In the meanwhile, if different objectives need to be achieved within the target groups, then place the most urgent at the top, followed by the others.

Table 4.1 Example overview of target groups and objectives

| Target Groups | Objectives |
|---|---|
| **Family doctors** | One month before its introduction, 80% of the family doctors in the Netherlands without their own pharmacy are aware of the side-effects of the medicine for heart patients. |
| **Cardiologists** | Six weeks before its introduction, 90% of the cardiologists in the Netherlands are aware of the side-effects Of the medicine for heart patients. |
| **Chemists** | One month before its introduction, 90% of the independently vested chemists in the Netherlands are aware of the side-effects of the medicine for heart patients. |

## Summary

In Stage 4, you determined the target groups and the communication objectives. You also determined exactly what you wanted to achieve within the target groups using communication. Within the target group analysis, you researched the characteristic of the target groups and where necessary, you segmented the target groups and measurably formulated the objectives for each segment. Subsequently, you gained agreement with the client regarding the target groups and objectives.

The preparatory work is now completed. In the next stage, you are going to determine the communication strategy.

## Stage 4 Sugro Group case study (continued)

*Target groups and objectives*

The firm Communication Partners (CP) is considering the Sugro Group's target groups.

- For the concern target groups, it would seem advisable to focus upon the financial target groups, particularly the investors and the financial press. This is obvious because both companies are listed on the stock market and, following the merger, their stock-market listing will be under a new name. In addition, the company also needs to be brought to the attention of the general public.

With respect to the internal target groups, the employees of both companies are equally important. In addition to the top management, middle management will also be involved in decisions relating to the new structure of the business. At this stage, no establishments will be closed which means that all establishments are of equal importance for the supply of information.



The approach is to emphasise the advantages that the merger will offer to both companies. Much is being asked of the employees (possible relocation) but no jobs are on the line. The Sugro Group is a good employer for its personnel.

The firm is now working on an additional effect which requires further investigation. What exactly are the communication objectives for each target group? These are broadly as follows:

- The emphasis relating to the concern and internal target groups continues to be placed on knowledge-based and behavioural objectives. Specific behavioural intentions are less important here as the main concern is to gain awareness of the newly merged organisation and the confidence of the investors. In addition, it is important that the employees understand the necessity and consequences of the merger and feel involved in the organisation as a whole.
- Behavioural intentions are certainly important for the commercial target groups. At this stage, the effect on the commercial target groups is still on the product category and the functional sweets. A

pilot is being carried out in order to gain ideas. At a later stage, a special campaign plan will be created for each new product.

Now that, broadly speaking, agreement has been reached, CP is developing the objectives further.

*To be continued ...*

# Stage 5 Communication Strategy

In the communication strategy, you describe how you are going to achieve the objectives you formulated in the previous stage. First you re-state the key idea, which is your outline approach and which describes the way in which the target groups will be approached and the positioning of the organisation or brand. Subsequently, you determine the central theme of the communication and the message for each target group. Naturally, you need to justify the choices made. Once you have reached agreement with the client regarding the key idea, you then develop this further by choosing the communication instruments.
In addition to all the knowledge and insight you gained in the previous stages, your creativity as a communication expert is indispensable when developing the communication strategy.

## 5.1 The key idea

What is your key idea for approaching the target groups? How are you planning to realise the communication objectives? You need to justify why certain choices were made and why the alternatives were not chosen. In your reasoning, confirm why you believe the communication objectives will be achieved more effectively and efficiently using your method.
Your key idea will differ for each situation, as it particularly concerns the approach and positioning. Furthermore, you need to provide a central theme and message for each target group (see Figure 5.1). A few examples are given below.

Figure 5.1. The key idea

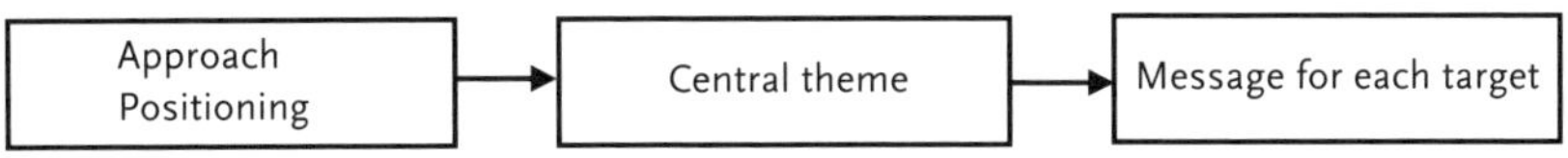

### The approach

The manner of approaching the target groups is not concerned with the contents of the communication but rather the form and style of the communication when approaching them.

When communicating with the target groups, you can strive for ***one-way*** or two-way ***traffic***, in other words, a ***dialogue***. If a dialogue with the target group is desired, then how are you going to encourage this in the communication?

In the case of internal communication, you can decide to what degree the communication needs to be top-down (top management provides the direction) or bottom-up (involvement of the work floor). Within a culture-change process, you can reveal inspiring ideas from employees. That is bottom-up communication. However, within a re-organisation, decisions need to be made from higher up, so this frequently requires top-down communication.



You can choose a rational or a more emotional approach. A rational approach works particularly well with subjects or products where people feel greatly involved. An emotional approach, for which humour, fear, surprise, and pleasure could be considered, is often preferred for subjects or products where people show little interest. When choosing an approach, knowledge about the target groups and their information needs is very important (Stages 3 and 4).

▷ Rational/emotional approach

**Tip 21**

When you work within a team, ensure that the team members complement each other. Try to prevent grouping people together who all have the same background and specialisation. A diverse team has added value. In any case, ensure that there is at least one person in the team who likes building-up relations because networking is very important but not everyone enjoys it. When compiling your team, also consider the requirements of the assignment and the competency present within the client company.

You can also choose a ***direct*** or ***indirect approach***. Who is the sender of the communication message? Is it the organisation, or is the communication going via ***intermediary organisations***? This choice depends upon the confidence that the target group has in the sender, the influence of the sender, and the accessibility to the target group by the sender. In this 'method of approach' example, you will also see that, when developing the strategy, you need to build upon the knowledge gained from the communication and target group analyses.

▷ Direct/indirect

An organisation can ***act pro-actively*** and anticipate events, or it can have more of a wait-and-see attitude and ***act re-actively***.

People who act pro-actively research changes in the environment and apply these changes to decisions necessary for their own direction. Acting re-actively means waiting to see what the other parties are going to do (e.g. market leaders or pressure groups) and only then making a move.

▷ Pro-active, re-active

What form of ***openness*** is recommended for this organisation or that subject? In the case of strong competition, a company may decide to withhold important facts about its production process or new products being developed. In the majority of cases, openness is really the best trading method. For example, in the case of an organisation being unjustly accused of fraud, trust can be built up by providing an open inspection of its working methods.

▷ Openness



**Tip 22**

Positioning is only worthwhile if all the personnel understand the concept and stand behind it. It must be clear to everyone what the organisation wants. Accordingly, it is essential that you firstly create an internal foundation, e.g. by presenting the plan or campaign.

You should also consider the ***style*** of communication for the target groups, that is to say, the 'tone-of-voice'. A business-like approach may be recommended for internal communication regarding a re-organisation, whereas for a culture change, it may be better to choose a somewhat more personal style when addressing this target group.

When choosing a style, you need to take into account the attitude of the target group with respect to the subject. Setting a one-sided promotional tone regarding a change process will not go down very well with a sceptical target group.

▷ Style choice, tone-of-voice

Concern communication can relate to a public-opinion issue. Within the communication analysis, you tracked the various phases of an issue. Is it still receiving little attention or is it clearly visible within the public groups? A particular issue phase can affect the choice of approach and the urgency with which it is handled. If, for example, the issue is barely visible to the target group and the urgency is not great, then a ***phased approach*** would be best. First of all, the subject is brought into focus. Thereafter, more substantial communication takes place, e.g., with supporting and opposing arguments.

▷ Issue management, phasing

Another example where phasing is important within communication is for crisis communication. In a crisis, all attention is initially focused on solving the problem and limiting the damage to the image by quickly and satisfactorily handling the situation. Apart from these short-term activities, you could subsequently consider how to build up confidence again by initiating new activities. These ***long*** and ***short-term*** activities must not collide with each other. For example, if some defective products need to be 'recalled', there is no point in starting a new communication campaign at the same time.

▷ Crisis communication



Within marketing communication, a product introduction or innovation requires a completely different strategy from that for maintaining brand recognition of a long-existing product. The key idea must align with the current ***life-cycle phase*** of the product. The objectives are different for each phase. This means that the strategy for achieving the objectives also needs to differ for each phase. With a product introduction for example, you could begin by choosing to increase product awareness and stimulate people into trying it out.

▷ Product introduction

Internal communication often requires a combination of line and parallel communication. ***Line communication*** utilises the hierarchical lines within an organisation. What is discussed within top management is translated by middle management as what is required for the employees of the various departments. You can relate this to departmental discussions within various levels in the organisation.

Usually, line communication is supplemented with ***parallel communication***, whereby all the employees are reached using the same means and message. An internal magazine is a good example. In the strategy, you indicate which of the above choices you wish to focus on and justify this.

As you can see from the above examples, there is always more than one way to approach the target groups. Which approach is best depends upon the intended objectives. You estimate which approach will be the most effective for achieving the objectives. Accordingly, it is about the ***effectiveness*** of the chosen strategy. In addition, ***efficiency*** is also important. Some choices will be made based upon the costs and budget available. Always relate your choice to the previously proposed priorities and urgency outlined in Stage 4 (target groups and objectives).

It is recommended that you propose various alternatives and subsequently provide a well-argued choice. Accordingly, you should also state why you did not choose the other possibilities.

### Positioning

One important aspect of the strategy is ***positioning***. How are you planning to position the organisation or brand in the market?

You choose your positioning by thoroughly analysing what the organisation wants, what the competition is doing, and what the environmental requirements are. Naturally, the positioning needs to align with the actual identity of the organisation or nature of the product or service. If you promise more than you can deliver, then people will be disappointed on introduction and that will ultimately be counter-productive.

▷ Positioning

When positioning, you need to place more emphasis on one particular characteristic of the organisation or product than on another. Furthermore, you need to ensure that there is a clear ***profile*** of the organisation or product.

A management vision is required for positioning. Additionally, the employees need to understand and support the positioning, otherwise they will not be able to convincingly communicate this when contacting the target groups. Accordingly, this requires good internal communication.

Positioning problems can operate at different levels and the term can be used to relate to different problems. It could concern the positioning of a brand (marketing communication) or, alternatively, the strategic positioning of an organisation. The latter forms part of the organisation's strategic policy. This choice has consequences for the organisation's products and services as well as for the way in which the organisation is organised. These positioning problems go beyond the working requirements of the communication expert (you have an advisory role within concern communication).

**Tip 23**
It is important to have regular contact with the client, even when there are no noticeable or startling developments. Is the client still happy with the progress of the project and have a good feeling about it? In addition to the agreed times, you can also meet between times and show informal progress results. Forwarding relevant messages from the media can be a good reason to make contact.

Within marketing communication, the positioning is that taken by a brand with respect to other brands. In order to differentiate a brand from other brands, you can either choose an informational positioning or a transformational positioning.
An ***informational positioning*** puts forward the communication, as to why the product or service is so good, in an informative manner. This is particularly relevant for receivers who make a rational comparison between different brands, e.g. (expensive) durable consumer goods.
A ***transformational positioning*** particularly concerns the brand's characteristic image and radiated lifestyle. In the communication, the brand is linked to values that are important to the target group, to emotions and to lifestyle. The brand is 'labelled', for example, as convivial and cosy, wealthy or safe. This positioning is frequently chosen for products or services where the user makes emotional comparisons when buying or where products have hardly any influence (for instance coffee and beer).



▷ Informational, transformational positioning

### Central theme

One important choice is that of the central theme. This needs to be aligned to the positioning of the organisation or brand. Within the communication, what do you now particularly want to focus attention on?
The central theme is an important ***guide*** for attuning all the different communication statements to each other. It increases the recognition, the emphasis, and the ***synergy*** of all the communication statements. Communication messages can differ from each other in form and accent, but the central theme must be present in all statements.

As a result of choosing a transformational positioning, a brewery could choose to associate its brand with a convivial and cosy theme. The chosen theme should be important for a long period. Different emphasis can be placed within short-term promotional campaigns aimed at various target groups, but the chosen central theme forms the main thread throughout all of the promotional campaigns.

**Tip 24**

As a communication expert, you will be involved with a number of company branches but be aware of the 'language' you use; your choice of words is important. You would use different words when speaking to jewellers than when speaking with engineers. Government officials express themselves differently to nurses. Accordingly, make prior adjustments and collect material about the branch and organisation in question. Ensure that you understand the jargon.

A central theme can also be determined for internal communication. In the event of a company re-organisation, emphasis can be placed on the fact that, due to interventions, the company can have a future again. This can increase the acceptance of (cost-cutting) measures.



For a police recruitment campaign, emphasis could be placed on having a sensible, non-aggressive attitude towards the work. By choosing this central theme, you focus upon the profession in a well-thought-through way. This theme then becomes the starting point for all messages directed at the various target groups in the campaign.

The central theme concerns the way in which the subject is to be approached. From what viewpoint should it be viewed? This is known as 'framing'. Take the following example. Some pressure groups want it to be known that genetically modified food is artificial and weird gruesome. Action is taken to cover a crop field with plastic and the demonstrators then walk around wearing white laboratory coats. The images of the action clearly demonstrate the pressure group's view without using too many words.

▷ Framing, theories of persuasion, persuasive communication

### Message per target group

The central theme is important because the ***messages*** for the different target groups are formulated within this theme. You arrive at a specific message for the various target groups by asking yourself which arguments appeal to which target group. The message is accordingly aligned to the expectations and characteristics of each target group (e.g. the level of education and information need). The target group analysis has provided you with the necessary information.

▷ Messages

Messages for various target groups can differ somewhat. However, if the messages have been formulated from within the ***central theme***, they will not diverge very much. This is important because people give and receive information from various sources. A message intended for a particular target group can also be read by another target group. Accordingly, the messages for the various groups must not be contradictory, but they can certainly have a different emphasis.

Imagine that a car manufacturer is striving to obtain a quality image for a certain brand. Both private cars and lorries are produced under that brand. A central theme within marketing communication is chosen for each product group, with comfort being central for the private cars, whilst functionality is emphasised for the lorries. Both are quality aspects.
Subsequently, the central theme for the lorries is translated into messages for the various target groups. The message for the lorry drivers focuses on the lorry's functionality, with its well-thought-out through fittings, as a 'home from home'. The message for the financial directors of the transport companies focuses in another way on the lorry's functionality as requiring very little maintenance so offering a good return on investment.



Within marketing communication, the most important brand equity formulated for the target groups is known as the ***proposition***. This is the promise that you make to the receivers. You empathise with your customers and you let them know what the brand or product can offer them. Accordingly, the proposition is a reproduction of that promise.

▷ Proposition

Subsequently, the proposition is translated into a ***creative concept*** which is the creative effect of the proposition. A creative concept needs to promote the proposition to the target group in as good and appealing way as is possible. The proposition 'be careful with fireworks' then becomes, for example, 'don't be a jerk, don't play with fireworks'.

The ***message per target group*** stems from the central theme and the objectives that you previously determined for each of these groups. You now need to formulate the message per target group that is central in the communication and produce this as an overview.

Table 5.1 Example overview of target groups and messages

| **Introduction of a new car** | |
|---|---|
| *Target group* | *Message* |
| Own employees | Details of the new car |
| Showroom employees | The plus points of the new car<br>Questions from the project team are welcome |
| Customers | Get acquainted with this new car<br>The plus points of the new car |

## 5.2 Communication instruments

What communication instruments should you use to promote your message to the target groups? It concerns choosing the instruments that will help you achieve the objectives as effectively and efficiently as possible. Usually, you would use a combination of different instruments so that a ***communication mix*** exists.



For the internal communication, you can now further develop the combined line and parallel communication choice that you previously made (the key idea). You need to use the hierarchical lines in the organisation for the line communication and focus upon all the personnel for the parallel communication. What meetings or assemblies are you considering and what internal communication media should you use, e.g. personnel magazine or Intranet?

▷ Line communication, parallel communication

In the concern or marketing communication, you could choose advertising, e.g. (state what types of medium you want to use), direct marketing, promotions, free publicity, sponsorship, events, etc.

▷ Communication instruments

You now need to further develop the instruments to be deployed per target group. You should specifically describe which media you intend to deploy for each target group. Here are a few examples.

- If one of your instruments is sponsorship, state which target groups you want to reach, what you want to achieve from the target groups, what form of sponsorship you have in mind, and what type of sponsorship objects would be suitable for this. As an example, art sponsorship presents a different contribution to the image forming than sport sponsorship.
  ▷ Sponsorship

- If you choose free publicity, state what target group and objective you want to achieve and indicate what media types need to be approached, e.g. daily newspapers, trade magazines, or public journals.
  ▷ Press contacts

- If you propose an advertising campaign, state what target group and objective you want to achieve and indicate what types of media need to be utilised, e.g. billboards or bus shelters, TV or newspapers.
  ▷ Advertising

- If your proposed approach is via meetings (e.g. for interactive policy), state in your plan which target group and objective you want to achieve with each session.



**Tip 25**
Try to consider the acceptance of your advice at an early stage and not just when your report is completed. Sometimes it is useful and even necessary to inform certain people (e.g. the chairman of the works council or a specialist) or departments (e.g. p&o) in advance and to consider their opinions about the plan to be presented.

In short, describe what the intended result should be for each of the deployed instruments. Subsequently, incorporate the target groups, messages, and instruments into an overview diagram (see Table 5.2).

Table 5.2 Example overview of target groups, messages, and instruments

| **Introduction of a new car** | | |
|---|---|---|
| *Target group* | *Message* | *Instrument* |
| Own employees | Details of the new car | Business meeting<br>Video<br>Intranet |
| Showroom employees | The plus points of the new car<br>Questions from the project team are welcome | Technical folder<br>Business meeting<br>Test-drive<br>In-house magazine |
| Customers | Get acquainted with this new car<br>The plus points of the new car | Direct mail<br>Invitation to showroom<br>In-house magazine |

Your choice of communication strategy has financial consequences. Accordingly, your decisions need to align with the preconditions stated in the analysis phase. In the next stage (stage 6, Organisation), you will work out the costs by producing a rough estimate.

### Summary

When choosing the communication strategy, you do not immediately specify the communication instruments to be used. Firstly, you present the key idea for approaching the target groups and then justify your choices. You state the positioning and formulate the central theme which is subsequently translated into a message for the various target groups. Only then do you develop the proposal to deploy the communication instruments. This is presented as an overview per target group which includes the communication mix.

## Phase 5 Sugro Group case study (continued)

*Communication strategy*

Communication Partners (CP) has been reflecting upon the key idea for approaching the target groups.

- Name recognition and confidence in the new company is central within concern communication. Generating media contacts is therefore the most important instrument.
- Both internal magazines are being combined to form a new personnel magazine. This will form the backbone of the internal communication. In addition, work is being done to create a new joint Intranet which will include short news bulletins.
- With respect to the marketing communication, the Group's functional sweets are initially being assessed. The introduction is mainly concerned with the distribution channels and the consumers, particularly chemists, pharmacists, supermarkets, and (parents of young) consumers. An informative approach is required because the target groups are not yet familiar with such products. The positioning must first focus on health. However, one must be aware of a too medically oriented style; functional sweets also taste very good! This aspect also needs to be included in the central theme. For the consumer introduction, the idea is to have a combination of advertising and joint promotions. In order to promote trying out the product, samples will be linked with other health products. It is mainly concerned in getting new users interested who are focused on their health. It is not really the intention to get existing customers to change over to this new variant (this would lead to cannibalism of the existing products).
- The pilot study is focused on the new pH-chewing gum. In addition, it is important to state that there is a latent problem for the consumer. The dangers of tooth decay are still not so well known. Perhaps it would be possible to work together with dentists (organisations). Seeing that 'avoiding uncertainty' is a growing trend, the message could be that this chewing gum avoids problems (sugar-free) or solves them (pH-normalisation). The proposition 'it tastes good and cares for your teeth' could be translated into a creative concept.

CP will initially discuss the above-mentioned choices with the client. Thereafter, the proposals will be developed further to form a communication mix per target group.

- When developing the instruments, a wide range becomes visible. Media contacts focused upon financial target groups do not only lead to editorial attention in the financial newspapers but also gain attention, via TV sponsorship, in programmes covering economics subjects.
- At this stage, the internal instruments should also be developed further. A newsletter needs to be produced which promotes the integration of the company divisions.
- What needs to be assessed for the commercial target groups is which form of advertising within which media would be the most effective. The new product can be brought to people's attention through editorial background stories in newspapers that focus on the target group. For the joint promotions, consideration is being given to linking with toothpaste. Also being considered is exactly how the 'sampling' should be aligned for this new product category. This will also include costings.

Again, discussions with the client must take place as to how this stage should be completed.



*To be continued ...*

# Stage 6 Organisation

In this last stage of creating a communication plan, you prepare for the execution of the plan. You describe the organisation whilst implementing the communication activities and creating an outline plan. Subsequently, you draw up an initial budget and clarify the project procedure, including the type of collaboration. Furthermore, you state how you are going to assess the intended results of the communication effort and evaluate the collaboration, including the concept tests and pre-tests. You then provide a clear explanation of all these items.

## 6.1 Planning in broad terms

In the previous stage, you stated your recommended strategy and the communication mix that you wanted to deploy. In this last stage, you need to plan when and what communication instruments to use. First, you should state the ***duration*** of your plan. If your plan is for the longer term, e.g. two or three years, then you can produce a generalised planning overview. However, the client will often want to know exactly what is going to happen in the short term. Accordingly, in addition to the generalised multi-year plan, you need to develop an annual programme, which contains the projects and activities for each month. When the duration of your plan is six months or less, e.g. when it relates to a short-term project, you need to state exactly when and what activities are going to take place during this period.



You can use two diagrams for this:

- the overview containing the communication mix from the previous stage (the strategy), with an extra column for time planning (see the example in Table 6.1).
- a programme giving all the sequential activities for each month. You could also possibly use this programme as a timescale (see the example in Table 6.2).
  ▷ Time plan

This initial time plan does not yet form a schedule, it only indicates when and which target groups will be confronted with which activities. At this stage, you do not include the activity preparations and the person who is going to execute the various activities. In short, you just provide an image of 'what is going to be staged' but not what needs to happen behind the scenes. The preparations will be included later in a schedule in the operational planning phase.

▷ Schedule

Table 6.1 Example overview of the communication mix with time plan

| **Introduction of a new car** | | | |
|---|---|---|---|
| *Target group* | *Instrument* | *Time* | *Frequency* |
| Internal employees | Video | January<br>February<br>March<br>April | 1 x<br>4 x |
| | Business meeting | January<br>March<br>May | 3x |
| | Intranet | December onwards | Continuous |
| Showroom employees | Meeting | Mid January<br>End April | |
| | Technical brochure | Begin January | 1 x |
| | Test drive | End January | 2 x |
| | In-house magazine | End February<br>End February | <br>1 x |
| Customers | Direct mail | End January | 1 x |
| | Invitation | Begin March | 2 x |
| | Showroom | | |
| | In-house magazine | Begin March | 1 x |

Table 6.2 Example of a sequential activities programme

| Introduction of a new car | | | | |
|---|---|---|---|---|
| *Time* | *Activity* | *Target Group* | *Estimate* | *Co-ordination* |
| December | Meeting | Showroom employees | ff 3,000 | Marketing department consumers |
| January | Video | Internal employees | ff 10,000 | Communication department |
| | Personnel magazine | Internal employees | ff 5,000 | Communication department |
| | Mailing | Customers | ff 7,500 | Marketing services department |
| | Invitation | Customers showroom | ff 12,000 | Showroom management |
| February | In-house magazine | External business relations | ff 7,000 | Communication department |
| March | etc. | | | |
| April | | | | |

## 6.2 Budgeting in broad terms

When budgeting, you outline all anticipated costs (plus the possible proceeds). When a policy plan has been drawn up for the longer-term, you need to include the anticipated costs for the first year and also provide an estimate of the costs for the remaining duration of the plan.



In general, it is advisable to clearly differentiate between personnel and material costs. ***Personnel costs*** concern the investment in time. Some tasks can be performed within the client organisation but other tasks must be budgeted for outsourcing.
***Material costs*** should be classified by nature, e.g. printing and placing costs. You can also state how much money should be reserved, per activity or per target group. This needs to align with the priorities determined in the strategy.

**Tip 26**

If a client wants to have your complete report in order to go through it and 'adapt it', then you could possibly face a dilemma. It is completely acceptable for your client to amend incorrect facts and conclusions. That must always be permitted. However, it is not the intention that nothing of your original report remains. Consider well in advance (if possible, with others from your account team) where your borders lie and what you find acceptable. It is still your report.

In your budget, you also need to include any ***general costs*** that may arise, e.g. from monthly meetings with the client and general travel and overnight costs. In addition, it would be wise to have a reserve so that this can be utilised for any unforeseen events that may occur during the course of the planning period.

Postage costs should be clearly stated. Furthermore, you need to have prior discussions with your client regarding the best way to set up your budget. Often, you may need to align to the way in which the organisation's administration department is organised.
Once the budget has been discussed with the client, you can treat it as a guiding element when subsequently executing the plans, as you now know how much financial support is available for the particular activities.
▷ Budget

## 6.3 Procedure

The procedure for executing the plan can take on many different forms. The form is dependent upon the complexity of the project, the role taken by the communication expert (consider the roles of the expert prescriber or the process facilitator in Stage 1), the decision structure, and the project participants. For example, do all the participants belong to the same client organisation or department, or are there more organisations or departments involved? Does it relate to a costly and complex project with a large risk factor for the organisation involved, or does it concern a relatively simple executable project? These will also be linked to questions concerning who has the final responsibility and who can take the decisions.



Accordingly, it is about designing a structure for the organisation of the project and its progress control. Communication projects always involve many people. How are these people going to work together? The structure that you develop states ***who*** is involved in the project, the ***discussion form***, the ***job divisions***, and the ***responsibilities***.

Frequently, an existing workgroup or project team that has been especially selected for this project will carry out the majority of activities.
In practice, you will come across many co-ordinating groups. A short overview is given below, but be aware that the denominations and specified tasks do not always correspond in every situation.

## Forms of collaboration

A ***steering committee*** is frequently established, particularly for large and complex projects where several organisations or departments are involved. Its members represent the participating organisations or departments. A steering committee is focused upon the progress of the process and operates on a strategic and managerial level. Project teams, workgroups, and account teams pass on accountability, with respect to the progress of parts of the plan, to a steering committee. Accordingly, a steering committee does not get involved with the more practical aspects of the project.

A ***project team*** is usually selected for a particular project with its members are selected for their expertise, in other words their knowledge and skills. Sometimes the client also participates within the project team which controls the progress of the project and is responsible for its execution, including the more practical issues such as outsourcing (partial) assignments to designers, text writers, and communication firms.

Workgroups have many shapes and forms. A ***workgroup*** is frequently focused on the tactical and operational level of a communication project. Various workgroups can be found within a large project where they are each given a specific job area. In the event of a re-organisation or a merger, one workgroup would be concerned with the house-style while the other would work on the internal communication. For complex projects, workgroups often pass on responsibility to a steering committee or project group. The composition of the workgroup can differ depending upon the objective and job area of the workgroup. Members of a workgroup can be chosen because they work within the same job area as the various participating organisations. However, they can also participate because they actually work within a divergent job area of that same organisation.



An ***account team*** focuses upon progress and execution. Its members are selected because of their expertise within the communication area. The team not only operates on a strategic level but also on a tactical and operational level. You will frequently come across the term 'account team' within the area of communication. The whole project is defined as 'an account'. An account manager manages the team and is responsible for the progress of the process, and the management of the budget. Above all, the account manager has a co-ordinating role with respect to the other members of the team.

With respect to external companies, the team often consists of consultants, the secretariat, and a traffic manager as well as an account manager. The ***(senior) consultants*** are responsible for the parts of the account that include all activities involved in the planning and effort for specific communication media. Examples of this are the preparation and realisation of the products (such as presentations, advertisements, commercials, and website) and budget management and research (such as concept tests and pre-tests). The ***secretariat*** supports the daily progress and provides administrative support. ***Traffic*** is concerned with the actual production (e.g. printing) and distribution of the campaign material, flyers, commercials, folders, etc. This is a linking and line function that is sometimes underestimated but is very important for the progress of the project.

Ensure that the tasks and responsibilities of the clients and account team are well defined. This also applies to mutually agreed job divisions between the account team members.
Agreements need to be made regarding:
- job divisions within the team;
- responsibilities within the team;
- what the team will do itself and what it will outsource;
- who will make agreements (and what are the agreements) with the service providers, including the research offices, printers, designers, and media.



**Tip 27**
Budget management is an important aspect of the service. You need to look at the direct costs but you should also consider possible indirect costs of the assignment (e.g. costs that may occur in later years, when you propose a house style in full colour). In cases of uncertainty, involving a financial adviser or financial department in the assignment is recommended.

### Discussion

In practice, it appears that the majority of discussions with the above-mentioned collaboration are focused upon the realisation of the ***project***. Accordingly, always include a few (more process-oriented) sessions with all concerned to assess the collaboration in your plan. This can then be considered as an interim evaluation. In this way, irritations can be prevented and it increases the long-term relationship between the project participants. In addition, you need to address the following issues. Do we have sufficient time, capacity, and facilities to bring the project to a satisfactory conclusion? Can we make use of existing facilities such as address files, post rooms, copying, and transport facilities? Is there sufficient support outside the organisation for any increased activities? Who can we call upon?

## 6.4 Research and evaluation plan

In the communication plan, you need to define how you are going to approach the evaluation and what research needs to be done. What is frequently being asked during or after a project is not only whether the intended objectives were achieved (the effect evaluation) but also whether the collaboration and project progress were successful (the process evaluation). Subsequently, you will be asked to provide a project progress report whereby attention is paid to a number of items, not only where things have gone wrong but also where successful actions took place or good decisions were made.

**Tip 28**

A couple of days after sending a memo or other document, call the client to check whether it has been received and if everything is clear. It is an extra service and, above all, you get the opportunity to hear their initial reaction.



What this actually means is that it must be known at an early stage how and what is going to be evaluated. Above all, this will also need to be registered. The set criteria and the measurable points in time form the basis of the evaluation. It would be wise to plan evaluation points in advance, particularly when it concerns complex projects or projects that extend over a longer period. Moreover, a number of organisations work with a fixed evaluation model and reporting system that states the frequency and form.

### Reporting model

It would be preferable to set out your report in a clear and compact format. The experiences would then be noted according to a fixed procedure. It is important to know in advance what points the evaluation is going to focus on. This means that you will be completely clear about the subjects to be discussed and you will have considered the measurable points in time and criteria on which the subjects are going to be evaluated. You can then develop a list of criteria and measurable points of time. This contains a general section which could be relevant for every project and a specific section that is only relevant for the particular facets of this one project. Discuss with your client which subjects are going to be discussed in the evaluation.

The measurable points in time are the time periods when the measurements are taken. By doing a comparative measurement at different times, you can relate the results to each other. In this way, changes become visible. The first measurement is done prior to the communication effort. These results are then registered as a so-called 'zero rating', against which the subsequent results can be offset.

▷ Zero rating

In your evaluation, you state how you are going to examine the intended results (effect evaluation). In addition, you determine how you are going to evaluate the collaboration (process evaluation). We will discuss this in more detail.

▷ (Effect and process) evaluation



**Effect evaluation**

Due to the fact that you determined the objectives for the target groups in advance (in Stage 3), you can take interim and retrospective measurements regarding the degree to which the intended results were actually achieved. You compare the results to the earlier zero rating. Additionally, the target group's appreciation of the activities can be measured. ***Effect research*** is important as it shows whether the communication effort and its associated budget has been well spent. Thus, with the effect evaluation, you also take the spending into account. Furthermore, the learning experiences gained from the measured results are important for the following communication projects. You learn new things with every evaluation: which segments worked well and which did not. The latter also applies for the second evaluation segment, the process evaluation.

▷ Accountablility

**Tip 29**
Take care with your presentation. Ask in advance how many people will be present and preferably bring two extra copies of the consultancy report with you. If you can, take a look at where the presentation will take place. It is always useful to have seen the location because you then have an idea of the set up (of the attendees). You can also see where you and your team colleagues are going to sit. Most importantly, always allow plenty of time.

### Process evaluation

Process evaluation occurs many times during the project. It is important to map out what has happened during the project. How will the collaboration be done? Did the process run to expectations? In order to record your experiences, a logbook can be used. Furthermore, group discussions and interviews with those concerned can also be useful. In addition to gaining retrospective learning experiences, a regular process evaluation is particularly important for timely guidance of the progress and collaboration.

In addition to the team's result measurements and ***process evaluation***, it could also be useful to reflect upon the personal functioning of individual members of the team.
By periodically describing your own input, you gain a better insight into your own personality, behaviour, strengths and weaknesses, your ambitions, and feasibility. Naturally, this ***personal evaluation*** is not intended for the client.



### Concept and pre-test

At this point, you can also state which communication instruments you envisage will require a ***concept test*** or pre-test. With a concept test you research the reactions of a limited number of people from the target group, to the way you plan to design a communication medium. For example, you can show a 'story board' of a commercial. This is a sketch of the story line on which people can react before the commercial is produced. If the concept does not appeal to people, you can make a timely change to the commercial's approach. A concept test is carried out, particularly when the approach is critical or when it concerns a relatively expensive communication instrument.

▷ Concept test

You can also plan-in ***pre-tests*** for the execution phase. A pre-test permits the communication instrument (which is produced but not yet distributed or broadcast) to be shown to a limited number of people from the target group. A pre-test is almost always done when you make an audio-visual or printed communication medium.

▷ Pre-test

Both test forms are relatively inexpensive to execute. They prevent you from spending too much money on the execution or distribution while the communication instrument is not satisfactory. They protect you from failure. Accordingly, you should also state in the evaluation plan which communication instruments you may feel require a concept test or pre-test.

**Tip 30**

When submitting your consultancy report, you can choose to give a presentation, but you can also choose to have an interactive session or meeting which particularly allows room for discussion. In the latter case, you would subsequently submit your consultancy report. Moreover, what is important is your assessment of the client's expectations.



**Summary**

In the subject 'Organisation', which is the last stage in the plan, you present a time plan and generalised budget. Subsequently, you enter into the procedure for executing the plan. You also state the way in which the results and process will be evaluated and what pre-tests and concept tests are required. You have now prepared for the execution of the plan.

## Stage 6 Sugro Group case study (continued)

### *Organisation*

Communication Partners is setting up the planning. The budget for the next three years is being drafted and the postage costs for the annual programme are being allocated per project and activity. The budget for each segment is taking form. Agreements have been made with the client with respect to the financial handling of the annual programme. The Sugro Group's financial department has provided the coding and stated the way in which the invoicing needs to be done (financial preconditions).

The proposed working procedure is being put in writing, whereby the accountabilities will be defined and the job divisions will be stated. A separate work group is being set up for the pilot focused upon the new pH chewing gum. In addition, the firm is specifying measurable points in time for the evaluation. Furthermore, the process evaluation is receiving much attention. For the advertising, it is envisaged that both a concept test and pre-test will be required, because it concerns a new product group. A pre-test will be carried out on the first internal newsletter regarding the merger and the resulting changes.

*This ends the case study*

You will find a second case study example at the end of this book.

# Towards the Operational Phase

In this book, we have shown you how to set up a good plan by utilising all the stages of the communication plan. A systematic approach does not always guarantee success but it certainly increases the chances. In any case, by having a well-planned procedure, you can be sure that no important stages will be omitted.

As previously stated, there are numerous ways of creating a communication plan. However, no matter what your approach, we hope you realise the importance of being aware of what you are doing and why you are doing it. If you can put forward good arguments to support your course of action, you will always be in a strong position.

Once the client has accepted your communication plan, you can move onto the operational phase. Accordingly, your work as a communication expert is not yet completed. You need to create an advertising plan, a direct marketing plan, or a sponsorship plan, whereby the budget is also further developed. During this phase, it is important to continue devoting sufficient attention to the client's progress reports.



The operational plans fill the gap between the communication plan and the execution of the activities. You develop concepts and translate the messages for each target group into visual, auditive, and textual communication statements. Perhaps this may appear to be the 'real work', but be aware that the execution can only succeed if you have a well-thought-out and comprehensive communication plan, because this forms the basis of the proceeding project.

# Case Study: Municipal Waste Policy

### Stage 1 The Assignment

A borough council evaluates its waste-disposal policy and ascertains from an investigation that citizens' waste contains a large amount of old paper.

The Department of Environmental Management considers this undesirable and requests the information department to make inquires regarding what contribution communication can make towards solving this problem. In this case, the briefing is given verbally. The information department confirms the assignment in writing and requests background information via a memo. The manager of the environmental department functions as the contact person for the information department employee who normally answers questions raised by this department. This employee has only worked with the information department for a short time and raises the question during a consultation with the information department.



### Stage 2 Situation Analysis

Some public relations officers want to directly focus more attention on this subject within the municipal communication channels. Others propose that an initial internal and external analysis should be carried out, due to the fact that the problem has a previous history. The latter occurs.

The council previously had a well functioning waste-paper collection system in each district. Five years ago, it was decided that the waste-paper bins should be removed and the system should be replaced with paper collections by local clubs. In this way, the council killed two birds with one stone: the waste-paper bins were expensive and the clubs needed money. Thereafter, the clubs were supported via a subsidised minimum price for old paper.
The council waste-paper bins were removed from the districts and instead, a weekly list appeared within the local newspapers council section giving

addresses and times when citizens could bring their old paper to the club of their choice. The list included sports clubs, cultural societies, churches, and schools.

Now that the municipal waste-disposal policy is being evaluated after five years, it appears from waste production measurements that ordinary household waste contains a greater amount of paper than previously was the case. People are putting paper more often with their household waste.

The public relations officers decide to hold qualitative interviews with various households. In addition, all telephone enquiries from citizens and comments from the past regarding this subject are being analysed. The information gained from this research is used for a swot-analysis of the waste system but this analysis does not produce a positive image.

The ***bottlenecks*** can now be ascertained. The municipal officers had assumed that everybody had a child at school or had connections with one of the clubs and therefore had easy access to these locations. However, it appears that this was not relevant for some household categories. There are also no signposts to the waste-bins at the relevant locations, so that outsiders have to search for them. Above all, convenience is important for many people and it is apparently too much to ask to look in the paper every week to find the relevant location and opening times. The current system works best for people with strong connections with one of the clubs concerned. However, the number of people for who this is relevant is falling (this can form a threat to the current system).



The ***policy objectives*** are now clear. Replacing the successful but expensive municipal waste-paper bins appears not to be a politically achievable solution. Council members see this as an inconsistent policy. Further explanation of the current system in the council section of the local newspapers would also appear to be insufficient. The public relations officers propose to explicitly involve the clubs in the problem analysis and in developing the strategy. They consider a dialogue to be essential in order to improve the system (compare interactive policy forming). In co-operation with the clubs, factors are mapped out that have a positive or negative influence upon the success of the paper collection. Increasing the accessibility of the collection points becomes the key objective.

## Stage 3 Communication Analysis

***Communication***, via the clubs, can play a role in explaining to those citizens who hand in wastepaper. In this way, the percentage of paper handed in by these citizens can be increased (e.g. members of a club, church or parents of schoolchildren).

However, the situation is different for people not involved with one of the participating clubs or societies and a combination of communication and improved facilities is required. In order to prevent these citizens putting their old paper with the household waste, collection points must be made available that are not too far away, are easy to find, and are frequently open. At least one club must be found in each district with easy access to the waste-paper bins. Discussions between the clubs and civil servants must realise this.

If this proves to be unsuccessful in some districts, then the previously compiled list of ***parties involved*** can be re-assessed. Are there other involved parties who can contribute towards solving the problem? Perhaps there are companies who are willing to place a publicly accessible paper container on their property. Despite the previous history, the ***information climate*** is still being seen positively: the willingness to co-operate is great.



The ***main communication objectives*** are to make it publicly known that the accessibility to the collection points has been improved and to encourage citizens to make as much use as possible of these collection points. With respect to the pre-conditions, the public relations officers point out that not only does the communication require a certain budget, but so do the improvements to the collection points.

## Stage 4 Target Groups and Objectives

Within the target groups, differentiation is made between the people involved with the participating clubs and those who are not. The latter is a diverse group of people. It mainly concerns older people, double earners without children, and people who holiday in the district.

Now you need to determine the ***objectives per target group***. It appears that these not only relate to knowledge objectives but also to attitude and behavioural intention. The first target group consists of citizens who have connections with the involved clubs or societies. They need to know where they can bring their old paper and have confidence in the accessibility to the collection points. Furthermore, they need to be prepared to bring their old paper to their club.

Once the collection points have been improved, it should be achievable within four months that this target group delivers at least 80% of their old paper this way.

With regard to the 'non-involved' citizens, their diversity becomes visible. The objectives are comparable, but the varying characteristics of the target groups require a different approach with respect to the facilities offered. For example, for older people, it is important to have local facilities so that they do not have to walk far with their heavy load. Alternatively, it is important for double earners that the facilities are available outside working hours. The desired situation for this target group will only be achievable after six months because the extra collection points first need to be realised. Furthermore, the desired target percentage is lower (60%) because this group currently hands in very little old paper.

## Stage 5 Communication Strategy

The public relations officers are now examining the ***key idea*** in the approach. For the people involved with participating clubs, these clubs form an important channel. The clubs are being asked what they think they will require in order to regularly distribute information about this subject. It appears they would like to have background-recycling stories made available so that they can include these edited articles in their in-house magazines. They would also like to have supporting publicity. In the information provided to members, the clubs can emphasise the financial advantages for the club if members deliver their old paper to them. Furthermore, schools could focus attention on waste separation during lessons so that the children can see the importance of it and may perhaps bring the old paper to school themselves.



The message here is: 'Help your club and the environment by bringing us your old paper'.

For those citizens who cannot be reached via the participating clubs or societies, distributing information regarding the new, more accessible collection points via the council section pages should be considered.
The message here is: 'Working together on a cleaner environment is now even easier as there is also a collection point for old paper in your district'.

However, these new collection points must be prevented from becoming so successful that the others are no longer utilised. All the clubs are happy to continue participating. Accordingly, all the information from the clubs must be quickly put in place. Additionally, the placing and signposting of the collection points must be quickly expedited. All the collection points will continued to be mentioned in the council sections of the local newspapers.

Clubs and societies play an important role when implementing the ***communication mix***. The weekly council pages will be utilised but reference information that does not frequently change can also be placed, for example, in the council's yearly calendar for household waste. This can also be consulted to ascertain the collection points for chemical waste. News about changes to the collection system can be distributed via the local newspapers and local broadcasting stations. The choice of media will be shown in a schematic overview of the media mix per target group.

### Stage 6 Organisation

Now the timeframe is determined: the ***main planning terms***. Communication via the clubs is the first issue. Other information will be distributed when the new collection points are functioning well. The costs are worked out in a ***budget*** and the ***procedure*** is assessed. The production of material for in-house club magazines can be outsourced to freelance writers. They can also produce the background stories for the council pages in the local newspapers. Press releases regarding the changes to the collection system can be written by the communication officers.



The measurable points in time are determined in the ***evaluation plan***. Last time it took much too long before the effectiveness of the changes were measured. In addition to the waste flow, the measured opinions of citizens will also be included in the proposal.

The plan for restructuring the paper collection is being submitted to the municipal executives for a definitive main-line decision. The execution will be carried out in the form of a project (according to an operational plan). The communication officers are not only deploying communication, but have also advised that the facilities be improved. By doing so, the accessibility of the collection points will be improved. This would not have been possible without the club discussions.

# Recommended Literature


DeFleur, M.L. and S. Ball-Rokeach (1989) *Theories of mass communication*, White Plains: Longman.

Fiske, J. (1990) *Introduction to communication studies*, London/ New York: Routledge.

Ferguson, S.D. (1999) *Communication planning; an integrated approach*, London: Sage.

Gurton, A. (1998) *Press here; managing the media for free publicity*, Hertfordshire: Prentice-Hall.

Grunig, J.E. (ed.) (1992) *Excellence in public relations and communication management*, Hilsdale: Lawrence Erlbaum.

Pelsmaeker, P. de, M. Geuens, J. van den Bergh (2000) *Marketing communications*, Harlow: Pearson Education.

Schultz, D.E., S.I. Tannenbaum and R.F. Lauterborn (1994) *The new marketing paradigm; integrated marketing communications*, NTC Business Books.

Stacks, D.W. (2002) *Primer of public relations research*, New York: Guilford.

Vos, M.F. and H. Schoemaker (2001) *Integrated communication; concern, internal and marketing communication*, Utrecht: Lemma.

Windahl, S., B. Signitzer and T.J. Olson (1993) *Using communication theory; an introduction to planned communication*, London: Sage.

# Index

# About the Authors

Marita Vos PhD (1956) is a communication consultant/partner at acc Ede. She studied social sciences and specialised in communication studies at Wageningen University (cum laude). Later she took her doctoral degree in the field of image policy. She has previously worked as communication co-ordinator with the association of universities in the Netherlands, VSNU, and as communication manager with the umbrella organisation NZf in the health care sector. She has written several books, one of which is *Integrated Communication*, also published by Lemma. She also lectures at the School of Communication Management.*

José Otte, Ma (1960) is a communication consultant at the Ministry of Justice. She studied Dutch and history of the press, propaganda, and public opinion at the University of Amsterdam (cum laude) and marketing Nima-B. She previously worked as manager communication with the Amsterdam Tourist Board and as public relations officer with the Amsterdam City Transport Company. For a number of years, she was a college tutor with the School of Communication Management.* She was also associated with the Forum of Communication and Journalism as a project manager.

Paul Linders, Ma (1953) built-up his experience within the commercial and consultancy sectors in the areas of marketing and communication. He is currently a tutor at the School of Communication Management* where he manages a consultancy company for third-year communication students. In addition, he is a consultant/partner in the Meander Group in Montfoort, who specialise in social enterprising. Paul Linders studied social sciences at the University of Utrecht and is working on a PhD thesis in public affairs.

* The School of Communication Management belongs to the Faculty of Communication and Journalism, which forms part of Utrecht University for Professional Education.